Ready-to-Use Music Reading Activities Kit

A Complete Sequential Program for Use with Mallet and Keyboard Instruments

Loretta Mitchell

HERITAGE MUSIC PRESS

A DIVISION OF THE LORENZ CORPORATION
Box 802 / Dayton, OH 45401-0802 / www.lorenz.com

Previously published
© 1991 by Parker Publishing Company, Inc.
a division of Prentice Hall, Inc.
West Nyack, New York

10 9 8 7 6 5 4 3 2 1

Library of Congress Cataloging-in-Publication Data

Mitchell, Loretta, 1951–
   Ready-to-use music reading activities kit : a complete sequential program for use with mallet and keyboard instruments / Loretta Mitchell.
      p. cm.
   ISBN 0-89328-156-5
      1. Music—Instruction and study—Juvenile. 2. Sight-reading (Music) 3. Music—Theory, Elementary. I. Title.
MT155.M57 1991
781.4′23′076—dc20   90-7286
                                                                                    CIP
                                                                                    MN

ISBN 0-89328-156-5

HERITAGE MUSIC PRESS

A DIVISION OF THE LORENZ CORPORATION
Box 802 / Dayton, OH 45401-0802 / www.lorenz.com

About the Author

Loretta Mitchell teaches elementary general and choral music for the Brainerd, Minnesota public schools, and serves as the district K–12 music coordinator. She has taught vocal, instrumental, and general music since 1973. A Phi Beta Kappa, summa cum laude graduate of St. Olaf College in Northfield, MN, she toured with both the St. Olaf Band and the St. Olaf Choir. She earned the Master of Science degree in Music Education from the University of Illinois at Urbana–Champaign.

Mrs. Mitchell's professional awards include a Graduate Fellowship at the University of Illinois, Minnesota Teacher of Excellence, Minnesota Honor Roll Teacher, Minnesota Professional Development Plan Fellowship, Brainerd Teacher of the Year, and Minnesota Classroom Music Educator of the Year. She has presented workshops and clinics for state music education conferences, and for administrators and classroom teachers across the Midwest. In addition, she has held the offices of vice president and president of Minnesota Elementary Music Educators K–8, and classroom music vice president of Minnesota Music Educators Association. She has served on the Commissioner's Task Force for Restructuring Education, the Department of Education Elementary Curriculum Rules Change Committee, and the Music Model Learner Outcome Committee.

Other professional resources by Mrs. Mitchell include *Music Reading Made Simple, 101 Bulletin Boards for the Music Classroom,* and *One, Two, Three . . . Echo Me!* She is a contributing author to the *Primary Teacher's Ready-to-Use Activities Kit.*

About This Resource

The *Ready-to-Use Music Reading Activities Kit* is a series of sequenced activities to help students master the basics of music reading. These activities involve singing and playing—hands-on application of music reading concepts. The goal of the *Kit* is basic music literacy for *all* students. Through the step-by-step activities, students of all abilities can experience the excitement of connecting music with a printed score.

For easy use, the *Kit* is organized into three sections. Section One, "How to Use These Activities Most Effectively," presents specific directions and suggestions for using the program. Section Two, "Student Activities," provides 150 reproducible worksheet activities for the step-by-step development of music reading skills. Section Three, "Teacher Resource Materials," includes answer keys and tests for the activities, suggestions for extending the learning experience, and a variety of reproducible teaching aids.

Special Features

Special features of the *Ready-to-Use Music Reading Activities Kit* include the following:

1. *Students learn music through music itself.* Musical examples provide the context for presentation and reinforcement of concepts. Familiar folk songs are complemented by newly composed songs. And a supplementary song book at the end of the *Kit* presents 14 additional songs correlated exactly to the scope and sequence of this series.

2. *Instrumental and vocal approaches are combined to teach music reading.* Students use singing and playing skills to learn, apply, and reinforce music reading concepts. Sight-singing and sight-playing skills are reinforced. Solfege and absolute notation coexist.

3. *The approach is simple and direct.* The basic philosophy is simply "learning by doing." The series of activities progresses slowly and methodically. Objectives are clear, and procedures are consistent.

4. *The series uses common classroom instruments.* The activities are adaptable to a wide variety of instruments, including electronic or acoustic keyboards and mallet instruments of many shapes and sizes.

5. *Activities were developed IN the classroom FOR the classroom.*

6. *Skills and concepts are "layered" in a systematic progression.*

7. *Activities are adaptable to various teaching styles and physical situations.* Learners can work individually, in small groups, or as a class. Students of many ability levels can be challenged in the same class period. Teachers may choose to use the entire sequence, or integrate selected activities with other methods.

How It Works

The following factors combine to make this series of activities unique and highly successful.

A standard rhythm sequence is used to present rhythm reading.

• Rhythm skills are presented in the context of familiar chants. Skills are extended to patterns, composition, and combined rhythm-pitch reading.

Solfege and absolute notation coexist.

• A traditional solfege pitch sequence is used as the basis for introducing absolute pitches on the treble clef.

• Movable do is used as the catalyst for teaching sharps and flats.

Hands-on application is the key.

• Students learn by "doing."

• Students use multiple skills: singing and playing, as well as composing, listening, reading, writing, and creative problem solving.

Higher order thinking skills are challenged and developed.

• Composition exercises are included in each pack.

• Creative problem solving exercises challenge students to use information in new ways.

The format is easy to use.

• 150 carefully sequenced activities are organized into 14 "activity packs."

• Activity pages are reproducible, saving time and money.

• Activities move forward in an overlapping progression of steps.

• New concepts are carefully combined with previous concepts for greater retention.

The entire series is success-oriented.

• Students are given positive feedback for each success, each page and each pack.

• A certificate and special bonus page are included at the end of each pack.

• Students' self-confidence and self-esteem grow with music skills.

• Tasks are simplified. Students of every level can succeed.

Assessment and accountability are built in.

• Exercises on each activity page can be used for day-to-day evaluation of student progress.

• Fourteen end-of-pack tests can be used for more formal and detailed assessment.

Teacher resource materials provide teaching suggestions, reproducible teaching aids, answer keys, classroom ideas, and a supplementary song book.

Music literacy for all students is an achievable goal. Through the *Ready-to-Use Music Reading Activities Kit*, more and more students will confidently say, "Read music? Sure I can!"

Loretta Mitchell

Scope and Sequence Chart

PACK 1	PACK 2	PACK 3	PACK 4	PACK 5	PACK 6	PACK 7
beat rhythm quarter note eighth notes	melodic direction sol mi treble clef G E	rest	la A	half note	do C	re D

PACK 8	PACK 9	PACK 10	PACK 11	PACK 12	PACK 13	PACK 14
high do' C'	fa F	dotted half note	ti B	movable do D'	sharps	flats

Contents

SECTION TWO: STUDENT ACTIVITIES • 9

CONTENTS

SECTION THREE: TEACHER RESOURCE MATERIALS · 161

1

How to Use These Activities Most Effectively

The Ready-to-Use Music Reading Activities Kit is a simple and direct approach to music reading. Section one explains briefly what you will need, how to plan for maximum benefits, and how to implement the program simply and effectively.

WHAT YOU WILL NEED

The program is ready for immediate use. Very simply, to help your students learn to read music, you need only this kit and some instruments.

The Kit

The *Kit* consists of 150 reproducible activities organized into fourteen packs and supplemented by extensive teacher resource materials.

Each page is designed to present new concepts and combine them with previous concepts. Instructions are stated in simple, direct terms. Verbal explanation is kept to a minimum. You may choose to evaluate student progress on a day-to-day basis and place your initials, a stamp, or other reward symbol on the page, a positive reward for work well done.

The fourteen packs are organized according to a specific rhythm and pitch sequence. (See the Scope and Sequence chart on page viii.) Each pack amplifies the positive reward system with a certificate of completion and a Pack Bonus Page. Bonus pages give students opportunities to have fun using what they have learned, working with partners.

Among the teacher resource materials included in the *Kit* are Pack Tests for each of the fourteen packs, answer keys, ideas for extending the learning experiences, and reproducible teaching aids including Keyboard Guides and a Supplementary Song Book.

Instruments

These activities combine vocal and instrumental approaches to music reading. They require pitched and nonpitched classroom instruments for students to play. The number of instruments you use is arbitrary. Students may use instruments individually, in pairs, or in small groups. When students work in small groups one instrument per group works very effectively.

Students may use mallet or keyboard instruments to play exercises beginning on page II-5. Wind instruments (e.g., recorders) can also be used, but fingerings are not included on the student pages. Suggested *mallet instruments* include chromatic songbells, resonator bells, step bells, xylophones, metallophones, and glockenspiels. Primary students will experience success more quickly with instruments that feature removable bars, and can be preset for specific pitches. Many teachers prefer rubber mallets to wooden mallets. Rubber mallets cut down on bell resonance and create an atmosphere in which every student can hear, sing, and concentrate. Some teachers encourage the use of two mallets, thereby giving students who have the ability the added opportunity to learn mallet technique along with music reading.

Students may use a variety of *keyboard instruments* including traditional pianos, and electronic keyboards, organs, synthesizers, and samplers. A reproducible keyboard guide (pages 203-205) can be used until students become familiar with key names.

Nonpitched instruments are needed also. Rhythm reading exercises require rhythm sticks most frequently. Several exercises encourage students to select other rhythm instruments. Common classroom percussion instruments, such as hand drums, triangles, tone blocks, and tambourines, will work well.

PLANNING FOR INSTRUCTION

This program is ready-to-use. The activities can be duplicated and distributed for student use immediately upon purchase. To achieve maximum benefits, however, consider the following suggestions for preparation and planning.

Preparation for the Program

Although early music training is beneficial, no background is required to begin this program. The *Ready-to-Use Music Reading Activities Kit* begins with basic elements of music reading and progresses slowly, step-by-step.

Because the activities are based upon common folk song material, it is extremely beneficial for students to know the songs prior to seeing them in print. For maximum success, teach the folk songs by rote as part of your regular classroom experiences. Students will more easily read notation when melodies are familiar.

Planning

When planning for instruction, teachers select course and age level for implementation, and consider scheduling options.

Ready-to-Use Music Reading Activities are published as nongraded materials. The following guidelines may help when selecting the *appropriate course and age level* for use:

a. The *Kit* is designed for use in general music programs, choral programs, and instrumental programs.
b. The activities are designed for students in primary through upper elementary grades.
c. The reading level and vocabulary are geared for independent reading by grade three and above.
d. Most teachers who use these activities with grades one and two students use a large group format (see page 4).

Scheduling music reading experiences for the school year offers many options. Following are recommended scheduling options:

- Use the activities for full class periods up to three times per week until students have reached the level or goal which you have set.
- Use one-half (or other portion) of the class period for *Music Reading Activities* and the other portion for other curriculum experiences.
- Use the activities once per week until students have reached the desired goal.
- Use the program for a concentrated week to introduce it, and once per week thereafter until students have reached the desired goal.

- Use the program for a concentrated block of time within the school year.
- Concentrate use (two or three times per week) early in the school year, and use the program once per week thereafter.

Once students have reached your goal, you may wish to consider several options:

a. Keep records of individual progress (see page 6). Use these records to determine starting places for individuals the next school year.
b. Send activities and instruments home with the students who have not finished. Establish "office hours" during which the students can have homework approved and receive new pages.
c. Set up keyboard and bell centers in the music room, hallway, or media center. Allow students to work independently during music class, lunch hour, recess, or after school.

To obtain maximum benefits of the program, plan to use the entire sequence of activities concentrated into one school year, or extended over the course of several school years, for each student. These activities may also be used to supplement the curriculum. For this use, select pages which are consistent with music reading objectives, and use in or out of sequence.

IMPLEMENTATION

This program can be self-administered. That is, students can follow the instructions themselves and proceed, page by page, through the entire series. To achieve maximum benefits, however, you may wish to consider the following suggestions relating to instructional format, scope and sequence, assessment, recordkeeping, accountability, and helping students succeed.

Instructional Format

These activities can be used in a variety of instructional formats, including traditional large group, small group, individual, or combination approaches.

The most common format is a *large group*. In this approach the teacher distributes one page at a time to class members. As a group, the teacher and students read and follow all instructions, practicing one exercise at a time. Class time is allowed for individuals to perform alone and in small ensembles. Special help is made available to individuals during large group practice periods.

Using the *individual format*, students read and follow all instructions themselves, completing one page at a time. Each student obtains the teacher's approval before proceeding to the subsequent page.

The *small group format* is extremely successful. Students work cooperatively in groups of three to four members. Each student has a particular role to fill in the operation of the group. The group's task is successful completion of the page objective. Students help each other so that all may advance to a new page.

Many teachers prefer to combine the benefits of more than one format. A *combination format* might begin with the large group approach as described above. After completing several pages as a class, the teacher may initiate individualized and/or small group instruction.

Scope and Sequence

Based on a common sequence of *rhythm* values, this series begins with familiar chants and uses a counting system familiar to most teachers. Rhythm reading is extended to pattern reading and writing, and combination of pitch and rhythm reading.

Meter signatures are not included in these activities. Exercises and songs contain bar lines, however, for several reasons:

a. The child needs "catch-up" points for the eye when reading, singing, and playing.

b. Some teachers use the series to teach meter.

c. Some teachers use the program with students who have already learned meter signatures. They instruct students to study each example before practice, determine the meter signature, write it in, and then count and play.

The *pitch* sequence is familiar as well. Beginning with *sol* and *mi*, the student learns to associate *solfege* with absolute notation on the treble clef. As the pitch sequence progresses, the student learns the entire C major scale in absolute notation.

The *do* key symbol is introduced in Pack 12. Should you wish to introduce this symbol earlier, page XII-1 can be isolated and used at any point in the series. Students can be instructed to locate *do* on the staff and mark it with the correct symbol. Movable *do* becomes integral to the scope and sequence only as sharps and flats are introduced in Packs 13 and 14.

The scope and sequence is followed again in the supplementary songbook, pages 209-223. Use this collection of reproducible songs to reinforce work in the classroom or for enrichment or remedial work outside the classroom.

Assessment

Assessment of student progress can occur in two ways: (1) informally on a day-to-day basis, and (2) less frequently in the form of End-of-Pack Tests.

Because of hands-on learning, the *Ready-to-Use Music Reading Activities Kit* provides opportunities for daily assessment of individual progress. By listening to individuals on a daily basis, the teacher can make *day-to-day progress checks*. You may choose to check student progress on every page, or at selected intervals throughout the series. Should you choose daily assessment, consider these suggestions to make the process efficient and manageable:

1. Be prepared to point out the portion of the page that you wish to hear without having to study the page. Take time to select several possible choices on each page prior to class time. A few minutes of preparation yields many minutes of productive time with students.

2. Make sure that you hear only what is necessary to determine mastery of a page—usually just a few measures.

3. Glance over written exercises quickly as the student is getting ready to play.

End-of-Pack Tests provide more thorough and formal evaluation of students' progress. See pages 181-198 for reproducible tests, answer keys, instructions, and scoring suggestions.

Frequent assessment may identify students who are progressing particularly well and students who are having difficulties. The teacher, upon diagnosis of difficulty, might use the scope and sequence chart (page viii) to refer students to specific review pages.

Recordkeeping

Just as assessment with the *Ready-to-Use Music Reading Activities Kit* can be formal or informal, so can recordkeeping. Informal records are automatically maintained as the teacher initials the approval blank at the bottom of each page. You may choose to keep more formal records, however, and (1) record scores from Pack Tests, or (2) record pages completed by students. With formal, dated records the teacher can see at a glance the progress which each student is making during a specified period of time.

Formal recordkeeping need not be time-consuming. Following is a four-step plan for maintaining accurate records with the *Ready-to-Use Music Reading Activities Kit*:

1. Determine how often you wish to obtain data from your students (e.g., once per week, twice per quarter).

2. Set out paper squares near the instruments on data collection day.

3. Instruct your students to (a) pick up a paper square when they pick up their instruments, (b) write their first name, last name, and current page number on the paper at the end of the class period, and (c) return the paper squares when they put their instruments away.

4. Record page numbers in a record book.

Accountability

The *Ready-to-Use Music Reading Activities Kit* provides a measuring device for music program goals. With individual progress records, the music specialist or classroom teacher can document not only w*hat individual students know*, but more important, *how individual students can use what they know about music.*

Helping Students Succeed

The scope and sequence of the *Ready-to-Use Music Reading Activities Kit* is designed for student success. By promoting positive attitudes and using motivational techniques, the teacher can increase each child's potential for success. Positive attitudes in the classroom work to eliminate competition between students and foster cooperation and self-motivation. The teacher can establish and maintain a positive classroom climate in which each student respects his/her peers' level of attainment.

Ready-to-Use Music Reading Activities are designed with positive reinforcement and motivation factors built in. Motivation features of this program, some intrinsic, some extrinsic, include:

- the teacher's verbal reinforcement
- the teacher's initials or other stamp of approval for each page completed
- End-of-Pack certificates
- End-of-Pack bonus pages
- a personal feeling of accomplishment with the completion of each page and each pack
- the privilege of performing for the class or in public
- self-confidence gained with improvement in skills
- the development of positive attitudes toward music
- the privilege of checking out an instrument to take home (See page 200.)
- badges, stickers, or certificates. It is recommended that such reinforcers not make distinctions between ability levels, but rather reward students for attaining goals within their own ability levels.
- good news notes
- the privilege of working with friends as partners or in small groups

Classroom Management

Using a number of instruments simultaneously in one classroom need not raise your blood pressure! You might consider one or more of the following suggestions for classroom control.

It is helpful at the onset of the program to establish and practice with the students a *silence signal* which means "Freeze, I have something important to tell you." Not only is it easier on your vocal health, but it establishes a consistent means of gaining instant silence and attention in the classroom. Some effective silence signals include:

- An echo clap pattern. It is recommended that you choose a very simple pattern for this purpose, and use it consistently. The teacher claps, the students echo and freeze.
- Turning off the lights. The darkened room means "Freeze." Instructions are given in the dark. When the lights are turned back on, students resume their activity.

It is important to establish concrete classroom rules for distribution, collection, and use of instruments. The following are sample instrument rules:

1. Always work in your own workspace.
2. Play only when you have permission.
3. Freeze when you hear the "silence signal."

2

Student Activities

- PACK ONE
  beat, rhythm, quarter note, eighth notes
- PACK TWO
  melodic direction, sol, mi, treble clef, G, E
- PACK THREE
  rest
- PACK FOUR
  la, A
- PACK FIVE
  half note
- PACK SIX
  do, C
- PACK SEVEN
  re, D
- PACK EIGHT
  high do', C'
- PACK NINE
  fa, F
- PACK TEN
  dotted half note
- PACK ELEVEN
  ti, B

- PACK TWELVE
  movable do, D′
- PACK THIRTEEN
  sharps
- PACK FOURTEEN
  flats

I-1   **Keep the Beat**

1. Chant this rhyme. Clap the beat as you chant.

Mary had a little lamb,
Little lamb, little lamb,
Mary had a little lamb,
Its fleece was white as snow.

2. Chant this rhyme. To keep the beat, clap once for each square.

Twin - kle,	twin - kle,	lit - tle	star,
How I	won - der	what you	are!
Up a-	bove the	world so	high,
Like a	dia - mond	in the	sky,
Twin - kle,	twin - kle,	lit - tle	star,
How I	won - der	what you	are!

I-2   **Keep the Beat**

1.   Chant this rhyme and clap the beat. Clap once for each square.

Cuck-	oo,	Where are	you?
Cuck-	oo,	Where are	you?

2.   Chant this rhyme and clap the beat. Clap once for each square.

Star	light,	star	bright,
First	star I	see to-	night,
Wish I	may,	Wish I	might,
Have the	wish I	wish to-	night.

I-3   **Words Have Rhythm**

1. Chant this rhyme and clap the rhythm. Follow the big stars and the small stars above the words.

☆ ☆	☆ ☆	☆ ☆	★
Twin - kle,	twin - kle,	lit - tle	star,
☆ ☆	☆ ☆	☆ ☆	★
How I	won - der	what you	are!
☆ ☆	☆ ☆	☆ ☆	★
Up a-	bove the	world so	high,
☆ ☆	☆ ☆	☆ ☆	★
Like a	dia - mond	in the	sky,
☆ ☆	☆ ☆	☆ ☆	★
Twin - kle,	twin - kle,	lit - tle	star,
☆ ☆	☆ ☆	☆ ☆	★
How I	won - der	what you	are!

I-4   ♩ **and** ♫

Each big star ☆ is now a quarter note ♩.

Each pair of small stars ☆ ☆ is now a pair of eighth notes ♫.

1. Chant these words and clap the rhythm. Follow the ♩'s and the ♫'s above the words.

♫	♫	♫	♩
Twin - kle,	twin - kle,	lit - tle	star,
♫	♫	♫	♩
How I	won - der	what you	are!
♫	♫	♫	♩
Up a-	bove the	world so	high,
♫	♫	♫	♩
Like a	dia - mond	in the	sky,
♫	♫	♫	♩
Twin - kle,	twin - kle,	lit - tle	star,
♫	♫	♫	♩
How I	won - der	what you	are!

2. Clap and chant the rhythm syllables. Say "ta" for every ♩. Say "ti-ti" for every pair of ♫'s.

Name _____   **Date** _____

I-5   **Discovering Rhythm**

1. Chant this rhyme and clap the rhythm. Your hands will copy the words.

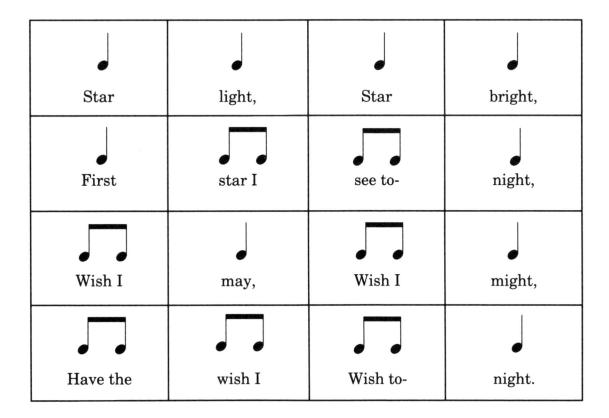

2. Chant this rhyme and clap the rhythm. Your hands will copy the words.

3. Clap and say the rhythm syllables. ♩ = ta   ♫ = ti-ti

I-6   **Writing Rhythms**

1. Chant this rhyme and clap the rhythm. Finish writing the rhythm above the words. Write one quarter note ___♩___ or one pair of eighth notes ♫ in each square.

♩	♩	♫	♩
Cuck-	oo,	Where are	you?
Cuck-	oo,	Where are	you?

2. Chant this rhyme and clap the rhythm. Finish writing the rhythm above the words. Write one quarter note or one pair of eighth notes in each square.

♩	♩	♩	♩
Star	light,	Star	bright,
First	star I	see to-	night,
♫	♩	♫	♩
Wish I	may,	Wish I	might,
Have the	wish I	Wish to-	night.

3. Clap and say the rhythm syllables. ___♩___ = ta   ♫ = ti-ti

I-7

Reading and Writing Rhythm

1. Chant this rhyme and clap the rhythm. Finish writing the rhythm above the words. Write one quarter note or one pair of eighth notes in each square.

♩	♩	♫	♩
One,	two,	tie your	shoe.
Three,	four,	shut the	door.
Five,	six,	pick up	sticks.
♫ Sev - en,	♩ eight,	♫ lay them	♩ straight.
Nine,	ten, a	big, fat	hen.

2. Clap and say the rhythm syllables.

♩ = ta   ♫ = ti-ti

I-8   **Names Have Rhythm**

1.   Chant these names and clap the beat. Clap once for each square.

♩ Rob-	♩ bie,	Dan-	ny,
♫ Car - o -	♩ lyn,	Jes - si -	ca

2.   Chant the names again. This time, clap the rhythm of each name. Your hands will copy the sound of the names.

3.   Finish writing the rhythm above the names. Write one ___♩___ or one pair of ♫ 's in each square.

4.   Clap and say the rhythm syllables.
      ___♩___ = ta   ♫ = ti-ti

5.   Think of names that match the rhythms below. Write the names in the spaces. Clap and say the names. Clap and chant the ♩ 's and the ♫ 's.

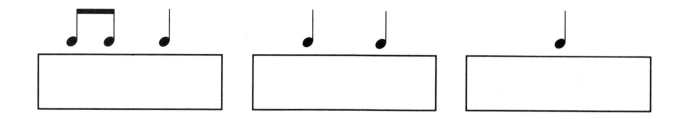

I-9   **Names of States Have Rhythm**

1.   Chant the names of these states and clap the beat. Clap once for each square.

♩	♩	♫	♩
New	York,	Wash - ing -	ton,
Ten - nes -	see,	Il - li -	nois

2.   Chant the names of the states again. This time, clap the rhythm of each state. Your hands will copy the sound of the names.

3.   Finish writing the rhythm above the states. Write one __♩__ or one pair of __♫__'s in each square.

4.   Clap and say the rhythm syllables.

__♩__ = ta   __♫__ = ti-ti

5.   Think of names of states, towns, or cities that match the rhythms below. Write the names in the spaces. Clap and say the names. Clap and chant the __♩__'s and the __♫__'s.

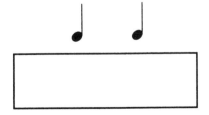

I-10   **Reading Rhythm Patterns**

1. Read and clap these rhythm patterns. ♩ = ta   ♫ = ti-ti

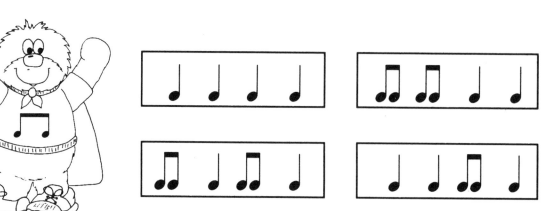

2. Write the correct rhythm syllables under these patterns. Clap and chant the rhythms.

♩	= ta	= one quarter note
♫	= ti-ti	= two eighth notes

I-11

A Matching Game

Clap and chant these rhythm patterns. Match each pattern with the correct rhythm syllables.

1.    ta   ti-ti   ta   ta

2.    ti-ti   ta   ti-ti   ta

3.    ta   ta   ti-ti   ta

4.    ti-ti   ti-ti   ta   ta

5.    ta   ti-ti   ti-ti   ta

6.    ti-ti   ti-ti   ti-ti   ta

I-12   **Playing Rhythm Patterns**

1.   Read and clap these rhythm patterns. ♩ = ta   ♫ = ti-ti

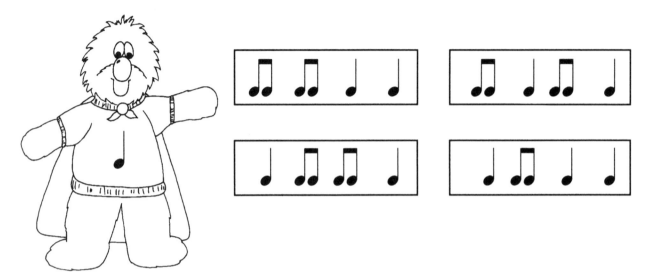

2.   Use a pair of rhythm sticks to play these rhythm patterns. Remember to say "ta" for every quarter note, and "ti-ti" for every pair of eighth notes.

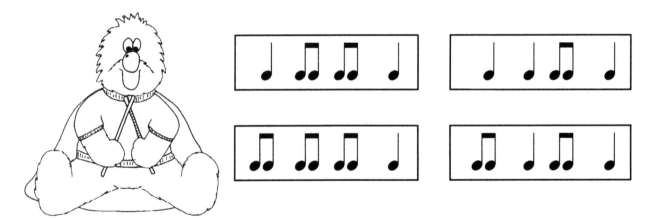

3.   Find a partner. You will each need a pair of rhythm sticks. Decide who will play one of the patterns above, and who will play the beat. Try to play both at the same time without getting mixed up. Exchange jobs and try again.

I-13   # Compose Your Own Pattern

1. Compose (make up) a rhythm pattern using ♩'s and ♫'s. Write your pattern in the squares below. Write one quarter note or one pair of eighth notes in each square.

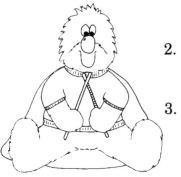

2. Practice clapping and chanting your pattern. Play your pattern on rhythm sticks.

3. Exchange patterns with a friend. Play your friend's pattern on rhythm sticks.

I-14   **Congratulations!**

You have successfully completed Pack One. Write your name in the box. Bring this certificate to your teacher to have it signed.

GOOD   NEWS

We are learning to read music.

> Write your name here.

has
successfully
completed
PACK ONE.

C   O   N   G   R   A   T   U   L   A   T   I   O   N   S   !

_____   _____
Date   Teacher's Signature

Pack One Bonus Page

Guess the Pattern
A Game for You and a Partner

Directions: Find a partner who has also completed Pack One. Choose a rhythm instrument. Decide who will be the player and who will be the guesser. The player will play one of the patterns below. The guesser will decide which pattern he or she heard. Exchange jobs. Play until each partner has had a chance to play five or more patterns.

II-1   **How Music Moves**

Music goes up, goes down, and stays the same. Printed music shows us when to play or sing higher and lower and when to stay the same.

Study these musical patterns. Look at the note heads to see how the music moves. Draw arrows in the boxes to show how the music moves.

 = UP   = DOWN   → = STAYS THE SAME

a.

b.

c.

d.

e.

II-2

Up, Down, and the Same

1. Study this printed music. Watch the note heads to see how the music moves. Finish drawing arrows to show how the music moves.

↗ = UP   ↘ = DOWN   → = STAYS THE SAME

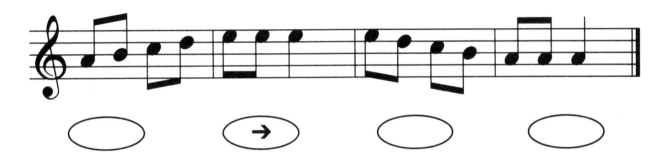

2. Study this printed music. Watch the note heads to see how the music moves. Finish drawing arrows to show how the music moves.

↗ = UP   ↘ = DOWN   → = STAYS THE SAME

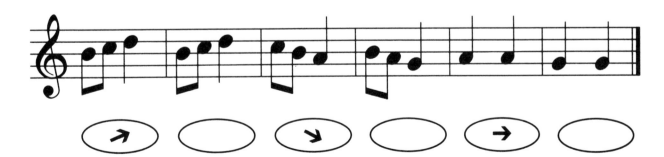

II-3   **Line Notes and Space Notes**

Printed music shows us when to play or sing higher and lower and when to stay the same. Musical notes help us to know how far to go up or down when we are singing or playing.

The heads of musical notes are made *around lines*,

or

in spaces.

1. These are line notes and space notes. Write an *L* under each line note. Write an *S* under each space note.

   L   L   S   L

2. Make up a pattern of line notes and space notes.

_____
_____
_____

II-4   # Singing Sol and Mi

Musical notes use the names of their lines or spaces.

These lines can be named *sol* and *mi*.

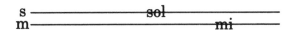

The notes around these lines are named
sol and *mi*.

1.   Your teacher will help you sing this song.

Cuckoo, Where Are You?

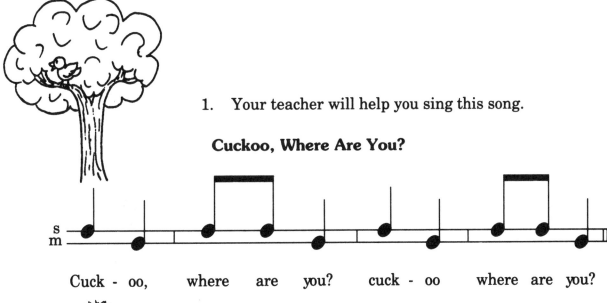

Cuck - oo,   where   are   you?   cuck - oo   where   are   you?

2.   Sing the song again. Sing the syllables *"sol"* and *"mi"*
     instead of the words.

II-5 **Sol and Mi on Bells or Keyboard**

The notes around these lines are named *sol* and *mi*.

sol   mi

Play this song on sol and mi. Sing the syllables *"sol"* and *"mi"* as you play.

Cuckoo, Where Are You?

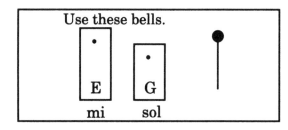

Use these bells.

E   G

mi   sol

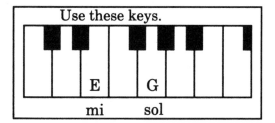

Use these keys.

E   G

mi   sol

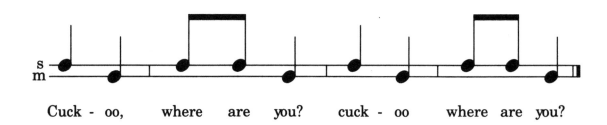

Cuck - oo,   where   are   you?   cuck - oo   where   are   you?

II-6   **Playing Sol and Mi**

These lines can be named *sol* and *mi*.
The notes around these lines are named
sol and *mi*.

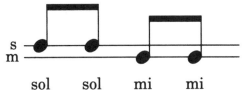

sol   sol   mi   mi

1. Study this song. Draw a circle around every ⊙*sol*.
    Draw a square around every ☐*mi*. Then sing the
    song.

Chickadee

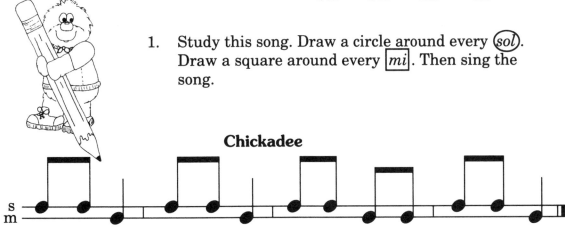

Chick - a - dee,   chick - a - dee,   can you sing a   song for me?

2. Play this song on *G* and *E*. Sing the syllables *sol* and
    mi as you play.

Chickadee

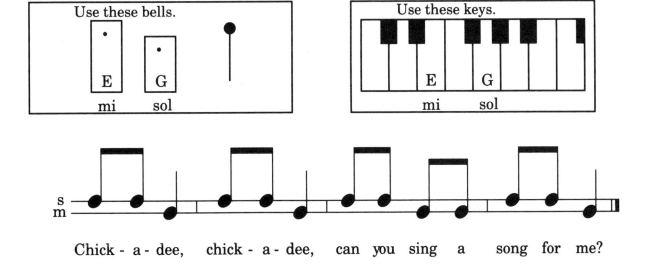

Use these bells.		Use these keys.
E	G	
mi	sol	E G
		mi sol

Chick - a - dee,   chick - a - dee,   can you sing a   song for me?

II-7   **The Five-Line Staff**

Music is often written on a five-line staff.

The lines and spaces can have *syllable* names.

do re mi fa sol la ti do¹

OR

The lines and spaces can have *alphabet* names.

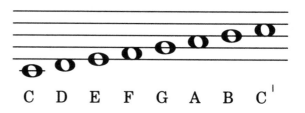

C D E F G A B C¹

1. Fill in the missing syllable names.

do re _ fa _ la ti _

2. Fill in the missing alphabet names.

C _ E F _ A B _

II-8   **The Treble Clef**

The lines and spaces can have

SYLLABLE NAMES   or   ALPHABET NAMES

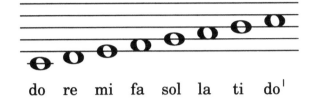

do re mi fa sol la ti do'

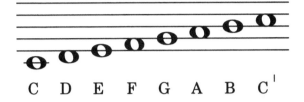

C   D   E   F   G   A   B   C'

The treble clef sign marks the *G* line.

1. Circle every *G* in this song. Sing the alphabet names.

Chickadee

sol

Chick - a - dee,   chick - a - dee,   can you sing a   song for me?

2. Play this song on *G* and *E*. Sing the alphabet names. Sing "ta" and "ti-ti."

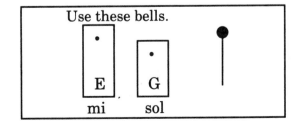

II-9   # Reading G and E

The treble clef sign
marks the *G* line.

The bottom line is *E*.

1. Play this song on *G* and *E*. Sing the alphabet
    names. Sing *sol* and *mi*. Sing "ta" and "ti-ti."

See-Saw

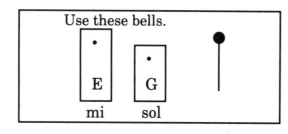

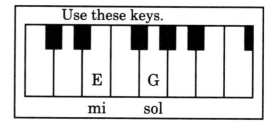

sol

See - saw,   smile   and   frown.   You   go   up.   I   go   down.

2. Draw a ♩ around the *G* line.
    Draw a pair of ♫'s around
    the *E* line.

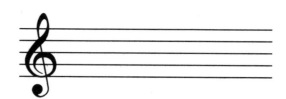

II-10

Practicing G and E

Sol and *mi* 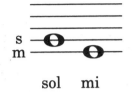 can also be named *G* and *E*.

sol   mi

G   E

1. Play this song three times on *G* and *E*. Sing the alphabet names. Sing the syllables *sol* and *mi*. Sing "ta" and "ti-ti."

School Is Out

School is out for to-day. Time to go out-doors and play.

2. Play this song on *G* and *E*. Sing the children's names. Sing the alphabet names. Sing the syllable names.

Calling My Friends

Rob - bie,   Car - o - lyn,   Jes - si - ca,   Dan - ny

II-11   **Playing G and E Songs**

Sing and play these songs.

Star Light, Star Bright

sol — Star light, star bright, First star I see to - night.

Wish I may, Wish I might, Have the wish I wish to - night.

One, Two, Tie Your Shoe

sol — One, two, tie your shoe. Three four, shut the door.

Five, six, pick up sticks, Sev - en, eight lay them straight.

Nine, ten, a big, fat hen.

Name _____ **Date** _____

II-12  # Composing With G and E

1. Learn to sing and play the first part of this song. Add notes above the words to finish the song. Sing and play the finished song.

The State Song

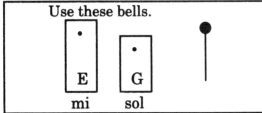 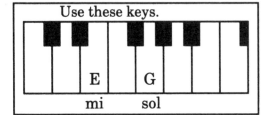

sol

New York, Ten - nes - see, Il - li - nois, Wash - ing - ton

2. Compose your own song. Make line notes on the staff below. Play your song. Sing *sol* and *mi*. Sing "ta" and "ti-ti."

_____
Write your title here.

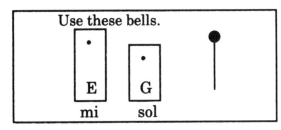 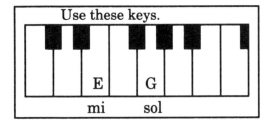

Name _____ Date _____

Congratulations!

You have successfully completed Pack Two. Write your name in the box. Bring this certificate to your teacher to have it signed.

G O O D   N E W S

We are learning to read music.

Write your name here.

has
successfully
completed
PACK TWO.

C O N G R A T U L A T I O N S !

_____   _____
Date   *Teacher's Signature*

II-14

Pack Two Bonus Page

Guess the Pattern—Game 2

Directions: Find a partner. Decide who will be the player and who will be the guesser. The player plays one of the patterns below. The guesser decides which pattern he or she heard. Exchange jobs. Play until each partner has had a chance to play five or more patterns.

III-1 **Learning About Rests**

1. Chant this rhyme. Keep the beat. Clap once for each square.

Peas	porridge	hot.	
Peas	porridge	cold.	
Peas	porridge	in the	pot.
Nine	days	old.	

Every word square gets one beat. Every empty square gets one beat.

Music has empty spaces in it.
Musicians fill empty spaces
with **rests**. A rest means
"quiet."

2. Draw a rest.

3. Draw a rest in every empty square in the rhyme above.

III-2

Reading Rests

1. Chant this rhyme and clap the rhythm. Throw your hands to the side and say "sh" for each **rest** ___.

♩ Peas	♫ porridge	♩ hot.	𝄽
♩ Peas	♫ porridge	♩ cold.	𝄽
♩ Peas	♫ porridge	♫ in the	♩ pot.
♩ Nine	♩ days	♩ old.	𝄽

2. Clap and chant the rhythm syllables.

   ___♩ = ta   ♫ = ti-ti   ___𝄽 = sh

III-3   **Writing Rhythm**

1. Chant this rhyme and clap the beat. Clap once for every square.

♩	♩	♩	𝄽
Ding	dong	dell	
Kit-ty's	in the	well	
♩	♫	♩	𝄽
Who	put her	in?	
Lit-tle	John-ny	Green.	
♩	♫	♩	𝄽
Who	pulled her	out?	
Lit-tle	Tom-my	Stout.	

2. Finish writing the rhythm above the words. Add one
    _____ ♩ , one 𝄽 , or one pair of ♫ 's in each square.

3. Clap and chant the rhythm syllables.
    _____ ♩ = ta   ♫ = ti-ti   𝄽 = sh

III-4   **Reading Rhythm Patterns**

1.   Read and clap these rhythm patterns.

 = ta    = ti-ti    =sh

2.   Write the correct rhythm syllables under these patterns. Clap and chant the rhythms.

 = ta = one quarter note

 = ti-ti = two eighth notes

 = sh = one rest

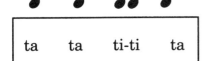
| ta | ta | ti-ti | ta |

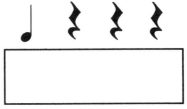

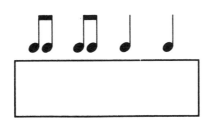

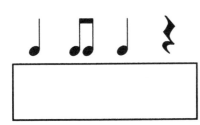

Name _____   **Date** _____

III-5      # A Matching Game

Clap and chant these rhythm patterns. Match each pattern with the correct rhythm syllables.

1.  | ta   ti-ti   ta   sh |

2.  | ta   sh   ti-ti   ta |

3.  | ta   ta   ti-ti   ta |

4. | ♩ 𝄾 𝄾 ♩ | | ti-ti   ta   ti-ti   sh |

5.  | ta   sh   sh   ta |

6.  | ti-ti   ti-ti   ta   sh |

III-6   **Playing Rhythm Patterns**

1. Read and clap these rhythm patterns.

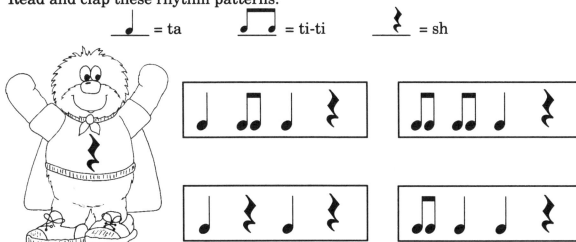

2. Use a pair of rhythm sticks to play these rhythm patterns.

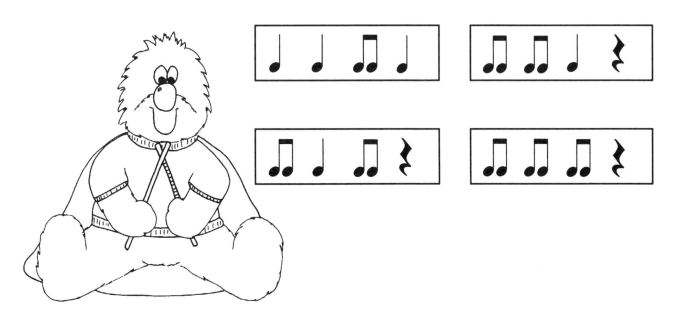

3. Find a partner. You will each need a pair of rhythm sticks. Decide who will play one of the patterns above, and who will play the beat. Try to play both at the same time without getting mixed up. Exchange jobs and try again.

III-7    **Compose Your Own Pattern**

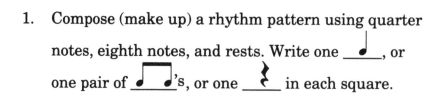

1. Compose (make up) a rhythm pattern using quarter notes, eighth notes, and rests. Write one ♩, or one pair of ♫'s, or one 𝄽 in each square.

2. Practice clapping and chanting your pattern. Play your pattern on rhythm sticks.

3. Exchange patterns with a friend. Play your friend's pattern on rhythm sticks.

III-8

A Song to Sing and Play

Play this song on *G* and *E*. Sing the words. Sing the syllables "*sol*" and "*mi*." Sing "ta," "ti-ti," and "sh."

Hide 'n Seek

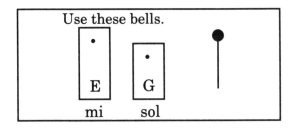

Use these bells.

E   G

mi   sol

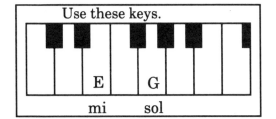

Use these keys.

E   G

mi   sol

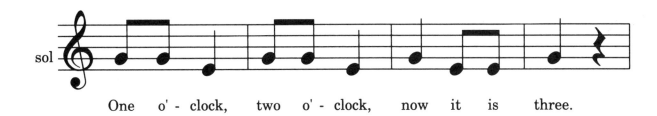

sol

One   o' - clock,   two   o' - clock,   now   it   is   three.

I   know   you're   hi - ding.   Where   can   you   be?

I   know   you're   hi - ding.   Where   can   you   be?

Name _____   **Date** _____

III-9   **Congratulations!**

You have successfully completed Pack Three. Write your name in the box. Bring this certificate to your teacher to have it signed.

GOOD   NEWS

We are learning to read music.

Write your name here.

has
successfully
completed
PACK THREE.

C O N G R A T U L A T I O N S !

_____   _____
Date   *Teacher's Signature*

III-10   **Pack Three Bonus Page**

Create a Pattern
A Card Game for You and a Partner

Directions: Find a partner who has also completed Pack Three. Choose a rhythm instrument. Cut these cards apart. Decide who will be the pattern maker and who will be the player. The pattern maker arranges any four cards into a pattern. The player plays the pattern, and says the rhythm syllables aloud. Exchange jobs. Play until each partner has had a chance to play five or more patterns.

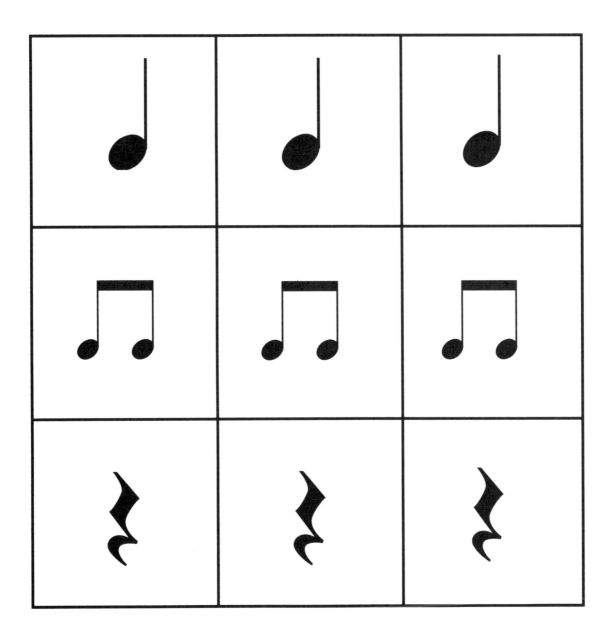

IV-1

Singing La

Musical notes use the names of their lines or spaces.

The notes around these lines can be named *sol* and *mi*.

A note above the *sol* line can be named *la*.

1. Your teacher will help you sing this song.

Rain, Rain, Go Away

Rain,   rain,   go   a - way.   Come   a - gain   an - oth - er   day.

2. Sing this song again. Sing the syllables *sol*, *mi*, and *la* instead of the words.

IV-2   **Finding La on Bells or Keyboard**

The notes around these lines are named *sol* and *mi*.

sol   mi

The note above the *sol* line is *la*.

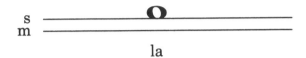

la

Play this song. Sing the syllables *sol*, *mi*, and *la* as you play.

Rain, Rain, Go Away

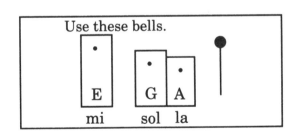

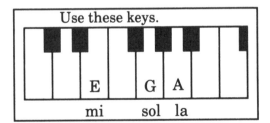

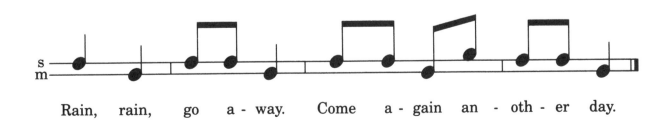

Rain,   rain,   go   a - way.   Come   a - gain   an - oth - er   day.

IV-3   # Playing Sol, Mi, and La

The notes around these lines are *sol* and *mi*. The note above the *sol* line is *la*.

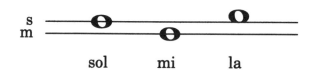

sol   mi   la

1.   Study this song. Draw a circle around every (*la*). Draw a square around every [*mi*]. Then sing the song.

Golden Fish

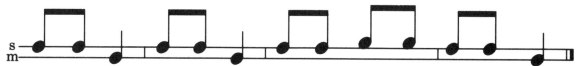

Gold - en fish, gold - en fish, Can you grant one gol - den wish?

l a

2.   Play this song. Sing the syllables *sol*, *mi*, and *la* as you play.

Golden Fish

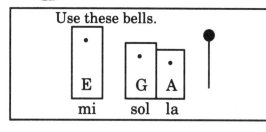

Use these bells.

E   G   A
mi   sol la

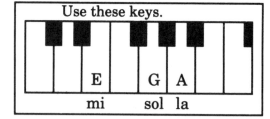

Use these keys.

E   G A
mi sol la

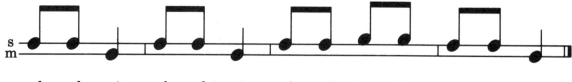

sol sol mi   sol sol mi   sol sol la la   sol sol mi

3.   Play the song again. Sing the rhythm syllables.

♩ = ta   ♫ = ti-ti   𝄽 = sh

IV-4   # Learning the Treble Clef

Music is often written on a five-line staff.

The lines and spaces can have

SYLLABLE NAMES   or   ALPHABET NAMES

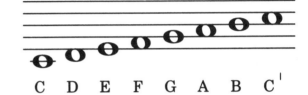

do re mi fa sol la ti do'   C D E F G A B C'

The treble clef sign marks the *G* line.

The space above *G* is *A*.

Write the alphabet name under each note.

G   A

IV-5   # Reading G, E, and A

The treble clef sign   marks the *G* line.

The line below *G* is *E*.

The *space* above *G* is *A*.

Play these songs. Sing the alphabet names as you play.

Golden Fish

sol

Gold - en fish, gold - en fish, Can you grant one gol - den wish?

Rain, Rain, Go Away

sol

Rain, rain, go a - way. Come a - gain an - oth - er day.

IV-6

Practicing A

The treble clef sign marks the *G* line.

The space above *G* is *A*.

1. Make a quarter note above each letter. Remember to make line notes *around* the lines, and space notes *in* the spaces.

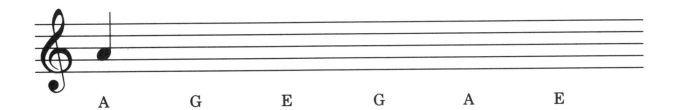

A   G   E   G   A   E

2. Play this song on *G*, *E*, and *A*. Sing the alphabet names. Sing the syllables *sol*, *mi*, and *la*. Sing "ta," and "ti-ti."

Bye, Baby Bunting

Bye, ba - by bunt - ing. Dad - dy's gone a - hunt - ing.

IV-7

More Practice with A

Sol, *mi*, and *la* 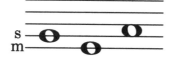 are also called *G*, *E*, and *A*.

sol   mi   la

G   E   A

Play this song. Sing the alphabet names. Sing the syllables. Sing "ta," "ti-ti," and "sh."

Lucy Locket

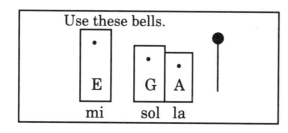

Use these bells.

E   G A

mi   sol la

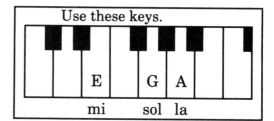

Use these keys.

E   G A

mi   sol la

sol

Lu - cy Lock - et   lost her pock - et,   Kit - ty Fish - er   found it.

Not a pen - ny   was there in it.   On - ly rib - bon   round it.

IV-8   # Composing with G, E, and A

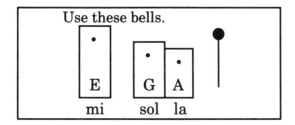

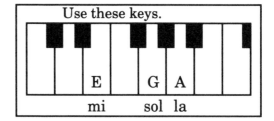

1.   Learn to sing and play the first part of this song. Add notes above the words to finish the song. Sing and play the finished song.

I Can Keep a Secret

I   can   keep   a   se - cret,   Keep   it   might - y   well

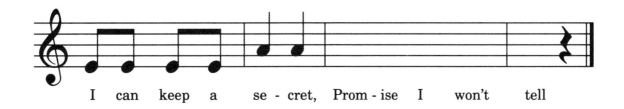

I   can   keep   a   se - cret,   Prom - ise   I   won't   tell

2.   Compose your own song. Make your notes and rests on the staff below. Play and sing your song.

_____

Write your title here.

IV-9   **Congratulations!**

You have successfully completed Pack Four. Write your name in the box. Bring this certificate to your teacher to have it signed.

G O O D   N E W S

We are learning to read music.

Write your name here.

has
successfully
completed
PACK FOUR.

C O N G R A T U L A T I O N S !

_____   _____
Date   *Teacher's Signature*

Name _____   Date _____

Pack Four Bonus Page

Create a Pattern—Game 2
A Card Game for You and a Partner

Directions: Find a partner who has also completed Pack Four. Cut these cards apart. Decide who will be the pattern maker and who will be the player. The pattern maker arranges any two cards into a pattern. The player plays the pattern and sings the rhythm syllables aloud. Exchange jobs. Play until each partner has had a chance to play five or more patterns.

Name _____ **Date** _____

　　　　　　Learning About Half Notes

1.　Chant this rhyme and keep the beat. Clap once for each square.

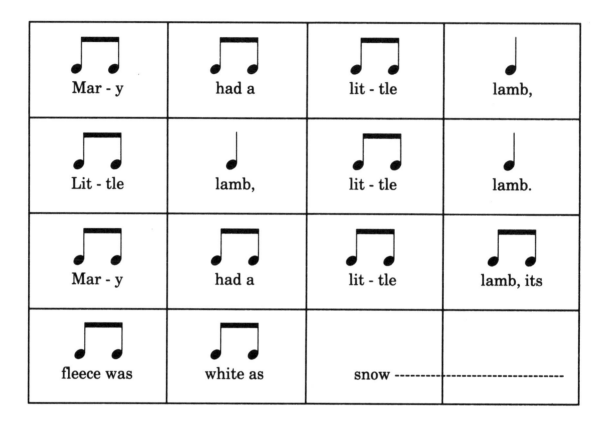

Mar - y	had a	lit - tle	lamb,
Lit - tle	lamb,	lit - tle	lamb.
Mar - y	had a	lit - tle	lamb, its
fleece was	white as	snow ------------------------------	

Every word square gets one beat. The word "snow" gets two beats.

Some words last longer than one beat.
Musicians can write longer sounds with
half notes. A *half note* gets two beats.

2.　Draw a half note.

3.　Draw a *half note* above the word "snow" in the rhyme above. Clap and say the
　　rhythm syllables.　

V-2

Reading Half Notes

Musicians can write longer sounds with half notes. A *half note* gets two beats.

1. Chant the words to this rhyme. Clap the rhythm. Hold each half note for two beats and say "ta-a."

Bell	hor - ses,	bell	hor - ses,
What's the	time of	day ---------------------------------?	
One o' -	clock,	two o'	clock,
Time to	go a -	way ------------------------------- .	

2. Clap and chant the rhythm syllables.

♩ = ta   ♫ = ti-ti

𝅗𝅥 = ta-a

Name _____   **Date** _____

V-3   **Writing Rhythm**

1. Chant the words to this rhyme and clap the beat. Clap once for every square.

♩♩	♩♩	♩	♩
Ring a -	round the	ro -	sy,
Pock - et	full of	po -	sies,
♩ Ash -	♩ es,	♩ ash -	♩ es,
All	fall	down ------------------------------- .	

2. Finish writing the rhythm above the words.
    Add ___♩___ , ___♩♩___'s, and one ___𝅗𝅥___ .

3. Clap and chant the rhythm syllables.
    ___♩___ = ta   ___♩♩___ = ti-ti   ___𝅗𝅥___ = ta-a

V-4   **Reading Rhythm Patterns**

1. Read and clap these rhythm patterns.

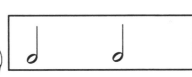 = ta    = ti-ti    = sh    = ta-a

2. Write the correct rhythm syllables under these patterns. Clap and chant the rhythms.

♩	=	ta	= one quarter note
♫	=	ti-ti	= two eighth notes
𝄽	=	sh	= one rest
𝅗𝅥	=	ta-a	= one half note

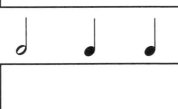

ta - a   ti-ti   ta

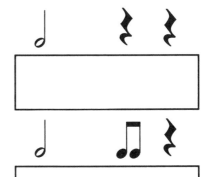

V-5

A Matching Game

Clap and chant these rhythm patterns. Match each pattern with the correct rhythm syllables.

1.    ta-a   ti-ti   ta

2.   ta   ~~sh~~   ta-a

3.    ta   ta   ta-a

4.    ti-ti   ta   ta-a

5.    ta-a   ~~sh~~   ~~sh~~

6.    ti-ti   ti-ti   ta-a

V-6   **Playing Rhythm Patterns**

1.   Read and clap these rhythm patterns.

 = ta   = ti-ti    = sh    = ta-a

2.   Use a pair of rhythm sticks to play these rhythm patterns.

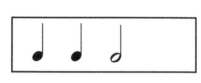 = ta   = ti-ti   = sh   = ta-a

3   Find a partner. You will each need a pair of rhythm sticks. Decide who will play one of the patterns above, and who will play the beat. Try to play both at the same time without getting mixed up. Exchange jobs and try again.

V-7  ## Compose Your Own Pattern

1. Compose (make up) a rhythm pattern using quarter notes, eighth notes, rests, and half notes. Write one ___♩___ or one pair of ___♫___'s or one ___𝄽___ in each square. Remember that a half note will take two squares.

2. Practice clapping and chanting your pattern. Play your pattern on rhythm sticks.

3. Exchange patterns with a friend. Play your friend's pattern on rhythm sticks.

V-8   **A Song to Sing and Play**

Play this song on *G*, *E*, and *A*. Sing the words.
Sing the syllables. Sing the alphabet names.
Sing "ta," "ti-ti," and "ta-a."

Bell Horses

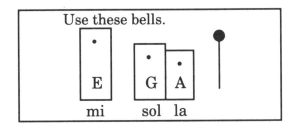

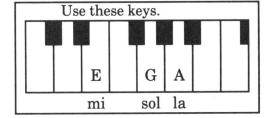

sol   Bell hors - es, bell hors - es, What's the time of day?

One o'- clock, Two o'- clock, Time to go a - way.

Name _____   **Date** _____

Congratulations!

You have successfully completed Pack Five. Write your name in the box. Bring this certificate to your teacher to have it signed.

G O O D   N E W S

We are learning to read music.

┌─────────────────────────────┐
│ *Write your name here.*   │
│   │
│   │
└─────────────────────────────┘

has
successfully
completed
PACK FIVE.

C O N G R A T U L A T I O N S !

_____   _____
       Date   *Teacher's Signature*

V-10   # Pack Five Bonus Page

Create a Pattern—Game 3
A Card Game for You and a Partner

Directions: Find a partner who has also completed Pack Five. Cut these cards apart. Decide who will be the pattern maker and who will be the player. The pattern maker arranges any two cards into a pattern. The player plays the pattern and sings the rhythm syllables aloud. Exchange jobs. Play until each partner has had a chance to play five or more patterns.

VI-1   **Singing Do**

These notes can be named *sol*, *mi*, and *la*.

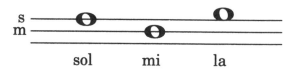

sol   mi   la

The line below *mi* is *do*.

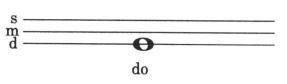

do

1. Your teacher will help you sing this song.

Peas Porridge Hot

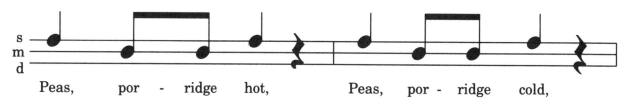

Peas,   por - ridge   hot,   Peas,   por - ridge   cold,

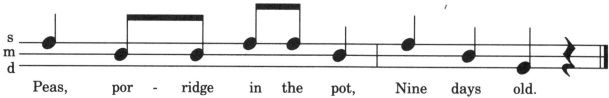

Peas,   por - ridge   in   the   pot,   Nine   days   old.

2. Sing this song again. Sing the syllables *sol*, *mi*, and *do*.

VI-2   **Finding Do on Bells or Keyboard**

The line below the *mi* line
is *do*.

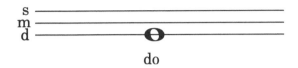

Play this song. Sing the syllables as you play.

Peas Porridge Hot

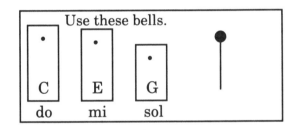

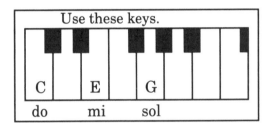

VI-3   **Playing Do**

The notes around these lines are
sol and *mi*. The line below
the *mi* line is *do*.

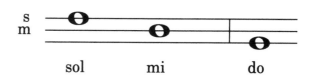

1. Study this song. Draw a square around every ⬜*la*.
   Find one ⓓⓞ and draw a circle around it. Then sing
   the song.

Mother's Calling

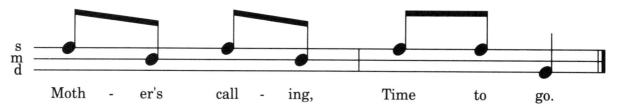

2. Play "MOTHER'S CALLING." Sing the syllables
   sol, *mi*, *la* and *do* as you play.

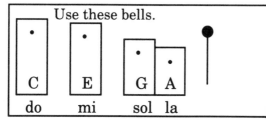

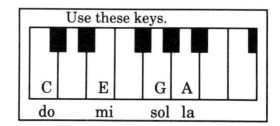

VI-4   # Learning the Treble Clef

Music is often written on a five-line staff.

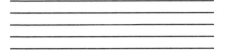

The lines and spaces can have

SYLLABLE NAMES   or   ALPHABET NAMES

 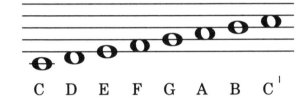

do   re   mi   fa   sol   la   ti   do'   C   D   E   F   G   A   B   C'

The treble clef sign
marks the *G* line.

A short line added
below the staff
is *C*.

Write the alphabet name under each note.

G

VI-5   ## Reading C

The treble clef sign
marks the *G* line.

A short line added
below the staff
is *C*.

Play this song. Sing the syllables. Sing the alphabet names.

Peas Porridge Hot

sol

Peas,   por - ridge   hot,   Peas,   por - ridge   cold,

Peas,   por - ridge   in   the   pot,   Nine   days   old.

VI-6

Practicing C

A short line added
below the staff
is *C*.

1. Make a half note above each letter. Remember to make line notes *around* the
   lines, and space notes *in* the spaces.

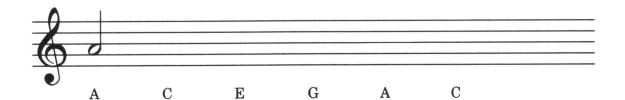

A   C   E   G   A   C

2. Play this song on *G, E, A,* and *C*. Sing the alphabet
   names. Sing the syllables. Sing "ta," "ti-ti,"
   and "ta-a."

Ring Around the Rosy

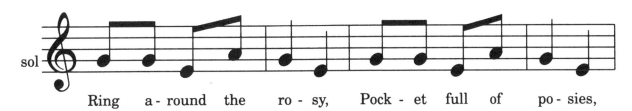

sol   Ring   a - round   the   ro - sy,   Pock - et   full   of   po - sies,

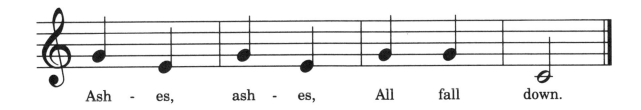

Ash - es,   ash - es,   All   fall   down.

VI-7   **More Practice with C**

Play this song.

Little Sally Walker

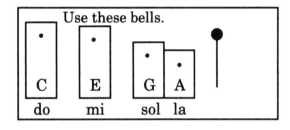
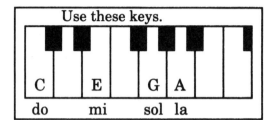

Lit - tle Sal - ly Walk - er, Sit - ting in a sauc - er,

Rise, Sal - ly, rise. Wipe your weep - ing eyes.

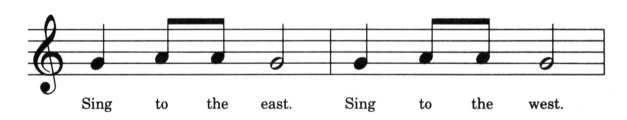

Sing to the east. Sing to the west.

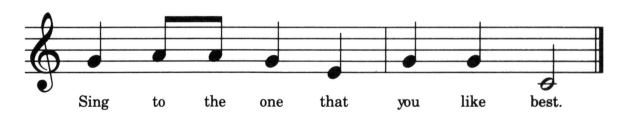

Sing to the one that you like best.

VI-8   # Composing with G, E, A, and C

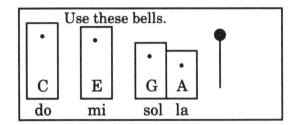

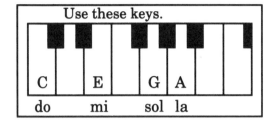

1. Learn to sing and play the first part of this song. Add notes above the words to finish the song. Sing and play the finished song.

Jack and Jill

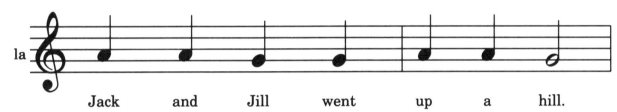

Jack   and   Jill   went   up   a   hill.

Did   they   know   they'd   take   a   spill?

2. Compose your own song. Make your notes and rests on the staff below. Play and sing your song.

_____

Write your title here.

Name _____ Date _____

VI-9   **Congratulations!**

You have successfully completed Pack Six. Write your name in the box. Bring this certificate to your teacher to have it signed.

GOOD   NEWS

We are learning to read music.

Write your name here.

has
successfully
completed
PACK SIX.

C O N G R A T U L A T I O N S !

_____   _____
          Date   *Teacher's Signature*

VI-10   # Pack Six Bonus Page

Name This Tune
A Game for You and a Partner

Directions: Find a partner who has also completed Pack Six. Cut these cards apart. Decide who will be the player and who will be the guesser. The player chooses one card and plays it for the guesser. The guesser listens to the song and tries to name it. Exchange jobs. Play until each partner has had a chance to play five or more tunes.

One, Two, Tie Your Shoe

Lucy Locket

Rain, Rain, Go Away

Little Sally Walker

Ring Around the Rosy

Bye, Baby Bunting

VII-1   **Singing Re**

These notes can be named
sol, mi, la, and *do*.

sol   mi   la   do

The space below *mi* is *re*.

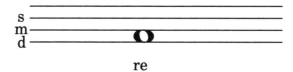

re

1.   Your teacher will help you sing this song.

Hot Cross Buns

Hot   cross   buns,   Hot   cross   buns,

One - a pen - ny,   Two - a pen - ny,   Hot   cross   buns.

2.   Sing this song again. Sing syllables instead of words.

VII-2   # Finding Re on Bells or Keyboard

These notes can be named
mi and *do*.

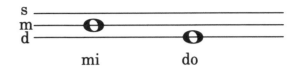

The space between *mi* and
do is *re*.

Play this song. Sing the words. Sing the syllables.

Hot Cross Buns

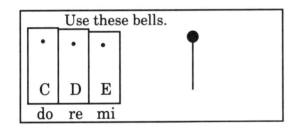

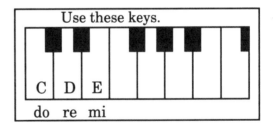

Hot   cross   buns,   Hot   cross   buns,

One - a pen - ny,   Two - a pen - ny,   Hot   cross   buns.

VII-3   **Playing Re**

The space between *mi* and *do* is *re*.

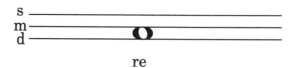

re

1. Study this song. Draw a square around every do. Draw a circle around every re. Then sing the song.

Sing Around the Campfire

Sing   a - round   the   camp - fire,   camp - fire,   camp - fire,

Sing   a - round   the   camp - fire,   all   night   long.

2. Play "Sing Around the Campfire." Sing the words. Sing the syllables.

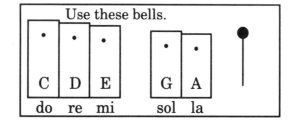

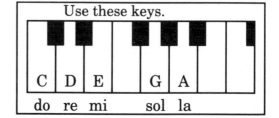

VII-4   **Learning the Treble Clef**

Music is often written on a five-line staff.

The lines and spaces can have

SYLLABLE NAMES   or   ALPHABET NAMES

   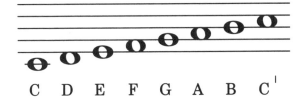

do re mi fa sol la ti do¹   C D E F G A B C¹

The treble clef sign marks the *G* line.

The space below *E* is *D*.

Write the alphabet name under each note.

A

VII-5   **Reading D**

The treble clef sign
marks the *G* line.

The space below
E is *D*.

Play this song. Sing the words. Sing the syllables. Sing the alphabet names.

Hot Cross Buns

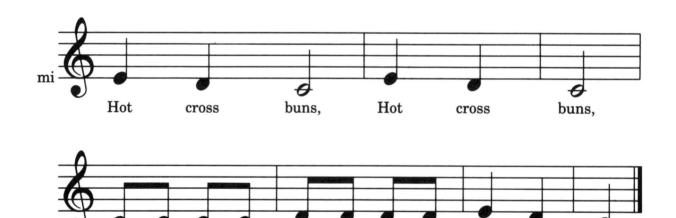

VII-6   **Practicing D**

1. Make a pair of eighth notes above each letter. Remember to make line notes around the lines, and space notes in the spaces.

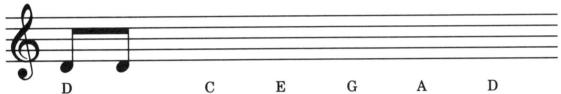

D   C   E   G   A   D

2. Play this song. Sing the words. Sing the alphabet names. Sing the syllables. Sing "ta," "ti-ti," and "ta-a."

Mary Had a Little Lamb

mi   Mar - y had a   lit - tle lamb, lit - tle lamb, lit - tle lamb.

Mar - y had a   lit - tle lamb, its   fleece was white as   snow.

VII-7   # More Practice with D

Play this song.

Rocky Mountain

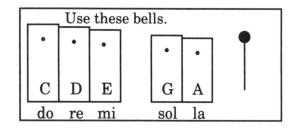

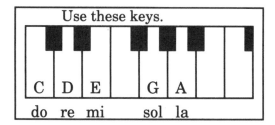

Rock - y moun- tain, rock - y moun- tain, rock - y moun- tain, high.

When you're on that rock - y moun- tain, hang your head and cry.

Do, do, do, do, do re - mem - ber me?

Do, do, do, do, do re - mem - ber me?

VII-8   # Composing with D

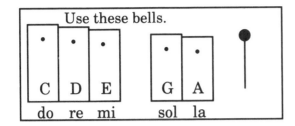

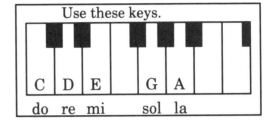

1. Learn to sing and play the first part of this song. Add notes above the words to finish the song. Sing and play the finished song.

Little Snake

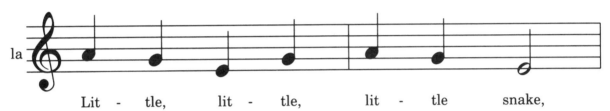

la

Lit - tle,   lit - tle,   lit - tle   snake,

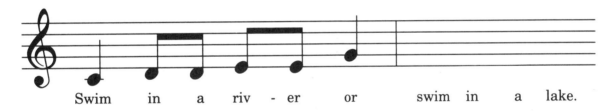

Swim   in   a   riv - er   or   swim   in   a   lake.

2. Compose your own song. Make your notes and rests on the staff below. Play and sing your song.

_____
Write your title here.

VII-9   **Congratulations!**

You have successfully completed Pack Seven. Write your name in the box. Bring this
certificate to your teacher to have it signed.

G O O D   N E W S

We are learning to read music.

Write your name here.

has
successfully
completed
PACK SEVEN.

C O N G R A T U L A T I O N S !

_____   _____
Date   *Teacher's Signature*

VII-10   **Pack Seven Bonus Page**

Make Up a Rhythm
A Card Game for You and a Partner

Directions: Find a partner who has also completed Pack Seven. Cut these cards apart. Decide who will be the pattern maker and who will be the player. The pattern maker arranges any four cards into a pattern. The player makes up and plays a rhythm for each note in the pattern. Exchange jobs. Play until each partner has had a chance to play five or more patterns.

VIII-1   # Singing High Do'

These notes can be named
do, re, mi, sol, and *la.*

do   re   mi   sol   la

The space above *la* is another
do. It is *HIGH do'.*

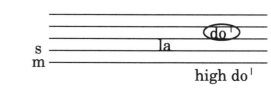

la   do'

high do'

1. Your teacher will help you sing this song. The start-
    ing note is *high do'.*

Bought Me a Cat

Bought   me   a   cat   and   the   cat   pleased   me.

Fed   my   cat   un - der   yon - der   tree.

Cat   goes   fid - dle - i - fee.

VIII-2   # Finding High Do' on Bells or Keyboard

The space above *la* is
high do'.

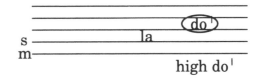

Play this song. Sing the syllables as you play.

Bought Me a Cat

VIII-3   # Playing High Do'

1. Study this song. Draw a square around every [low do]. Draw a circle around every (high do'). Sing and play the song.

Seashells, Seashells

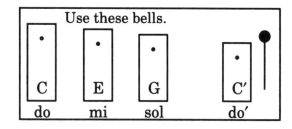

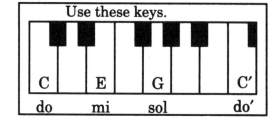

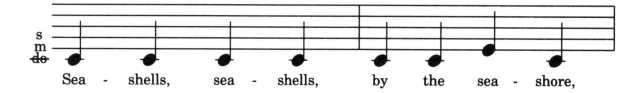

Sea - shells,   sea - shells,   by   the   sea - shore,

Find   a   shell   or   buy   a   shell,   by   the   sea - shore.

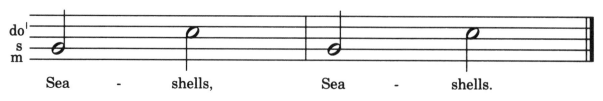

Sea - shells,   Sea - shells.

2. Play "Seashells, Seashells" as a round. Choose a partner. Decide who will start playing first. Player #2 starts when player #1 gets to the *. Each player plays the whole song two times.

VIII-4   **Learning the Treble Clef**

Music is often written on a five-line staff.

The lines and spaces can have

SYLLABLE NAMES   or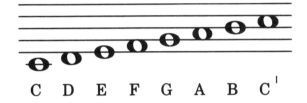

ALPHABET NAMES

do re mi fa sol la ti do'   C D E F G A B C'

The treble clef sign
marks the *G* line.

The space above
A is *high C'*.

high C'

Write the alphabet name under each note.

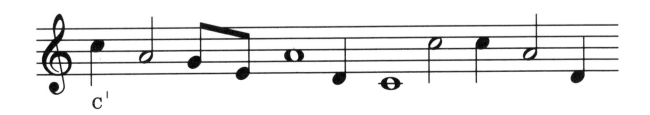

C'

VIII-5   # Reading High C'

The space above
A is *high C'*.

high C'

Play this song. Sing the alphabet names. Sing the
words.

Bought Me a Cat

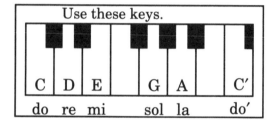

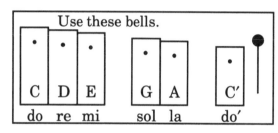

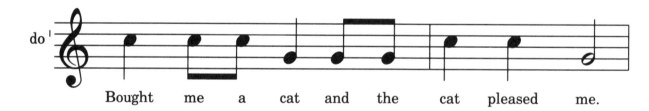

Bought   me   a   cat   and   the   cat   pleased   me.

Fed   my   cat   un - der   yon - der   tree.

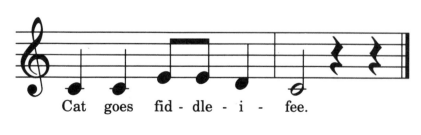

Cat   goes   fid - dle - i - fee.

VIII-6   # Practicing High C′

1. Make a quarter note above each letter. Remember to make line notes *around* the lines, and space notes *in* the spaces.

G   high C′   E   A   high C′   D

2. Play this song. Sing the alphabet names. Sing the rhythm syllables.

When the Train Comes Along

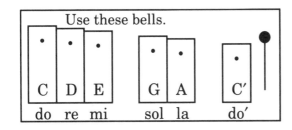

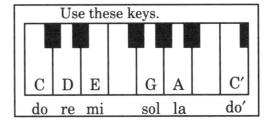

When the   train   comes   a - long,   when   the   train   comes   a- long,

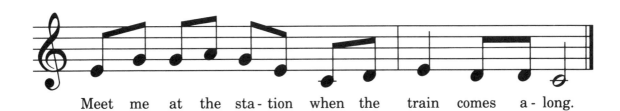

Meet   me   at   the   sta - tion   when   the   train   comes   a - long.

More Practice with High C′

Play this song. Sing the words. Sing the alphabet names.

Tidee-O

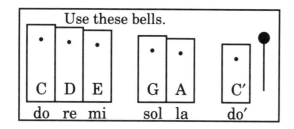

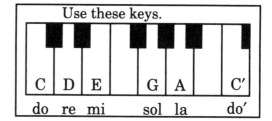

Pass one win-dow, Ti - dee - o. Pass two win dows, Ti - dee - o.

Pass three win - dows, Ti - dee - o. Close that win-dow, Ti - dee - o.

Ti - dee - o, Ti - dee - o, Close that win-dow, Ti - dee - o.

Ti - dee - o, Ti - dee - o, Close that win-dow, Ti - dee - o.

VIII-8   # Composing with High C′

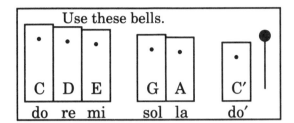

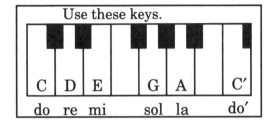

1. Learn to sing and play the first part of this song. Add notes above the words to finish the song. Sing and play the finished song.

Gotta Get a Puppy Dog

Got - ta   get   a   pup - py - dog,   noth - ing   else   will   do.

Got - ta   get   a   pup - py - dog,   how   'bout   you?

2. Compose your own song. Make your notes and rests on the staff below. Play and sing your song.

_____
Write your title here.

Name _____ **Date** _____

VIII-9   **Congratulations!**

You have successfully completed Pack Eight. Write your name in the box. Bring this certificate to your teacher to have it signed.

G O O D   N E W S

We are learning to read music.

Write your name here.

has
successfully
completed
PACK EIGHT.

C O N G R A T U L A T I O N S !

_____   _____
Date   *Teacher's Signature*

VIII-10   ## Pack Eight Bonus Page

Name This Tune
A Game for You and a Partner

Directions: Find a partner who has also completed Pack Eight. Cut these cards apart. Decide who will be the player and who will be the guesser. The player chooses one card and plays it for the guesser. The guesser listens to the song and tries to name it. Exchange jobs. Play until each partner has had a chance to play five or more tunes.

IX-1   **Singing Fa**

These notes can be named
do, re, mi, sol, la, and
high do'.

do   re   mi   sol   la   do'

The space between *sol* and *mi*
is *fa*.

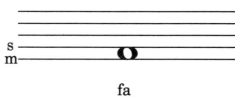

fa

Your teacher will help you sing this song.

This Old Man

This old man,   He played one,   He played nick - nack   on my thumb,

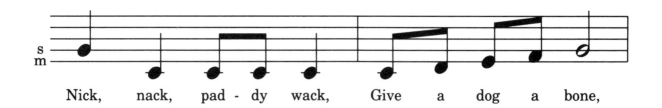

Nick,   nack,   pad - dy   wack,   Give   a   dog   a   bone,

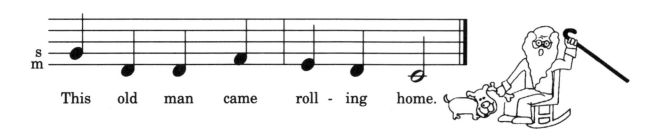

This   old   man   came   roll - ing   home.

IX-2   # Finding Fa on Bells or Keyboard

The space between *sol* and *mi*
is *fa*.

fa

Play this song. Sing the syllables as you play.

This Old Man

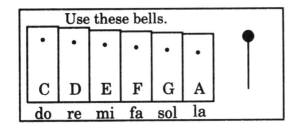

Use these bells.

C D E F G A
do re mi fa sol la

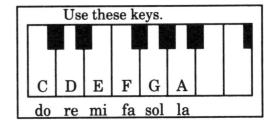

Use these keys.

C D E F G A
do re mi fa sol la

This old man,   He played one,   He played nick - nack   on   my thumb,

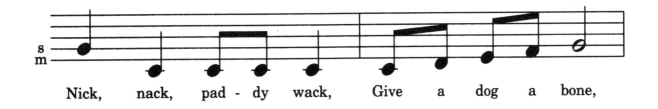

Nick,   nack,   pad - dy   wack,   Give   a   dog   a   bone,

This   old   man   came   roll - ing   home.

IX-3   **Playing Fa**

The space between *sol* and *mi*
is *fa*.

fa

1. Study this song. Draw a square around every
    [re]. Draw a circle around every (fa). Then sing the
    song.

Love Somebody

Love some - bod - y,   yes, I do. Love some - bod - y,   yes,   I do.

Love some- bod - y,   yes, I do. Love some- bod - y but I   won't tell who.

2. Play "Love Somebody." Sing the syllables as you
    play.

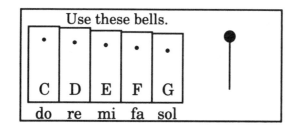

Name _____ **Date** _____

Learning the Treble Clef

Music is often written on a five-line staff.

The lines and spaces can have

SYLLABLE NAMES   or   ALPHABET NAMES

   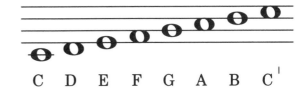

do re mi fa sol la ti do¹   C D E F G A B C¹

The treble clef sign
marks the *G* line.

The bottom
space is *F*.

Write the alphabet name under each note.

G C D

IX-5   **Reading F**

The bottom
space is *F*.

Play this song. Sing the alphabet names. Sing the
words. Sing the syllables.

This Old Man

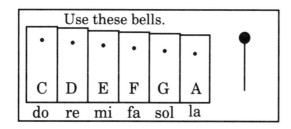

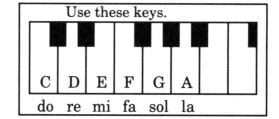

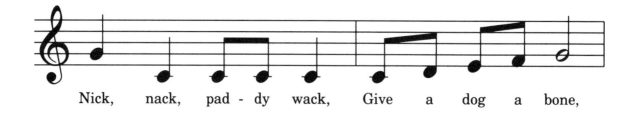

This old man, He played one, He played nick-nack on my thumb,

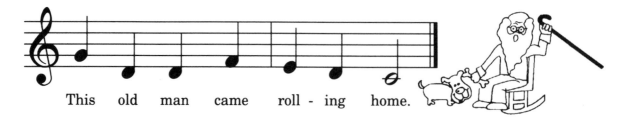

Nick,   nack,   pad - dy wack,   Give   a   dog   a   bone,

This   old   man   came   roll - ing   home.

IX-6   **Practicing F**

1.   Make a half note above each letter.

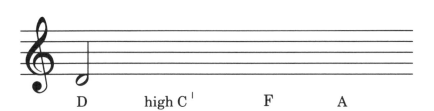

D   high C | F   A

2.   Play this song. Sing the alphabet names. Sing the syllables.

Twinkle, Twinkle, Little Star

Twin - kle, twin - kle,   lit - tle star,   how   I   won - der   what you   are.

Up   a - bove the   world so high,   Like   a   dia - mond   in the sky,

Twin - kle, twin - kle   lit - tle star,   how   I   won - der   what you   are.

IX-7   **More Practice with F**

Play this song.

Bluebird, Bluebird

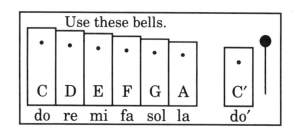
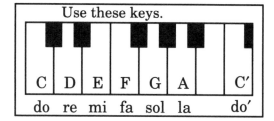

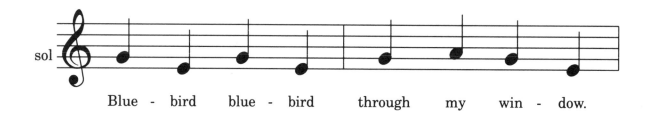

Blue - bird   blue - bird   through   my   win - dow.

Blue - bird   blue - bird   through   my   win - dow.

Blue - bird   blue - bird   through   my   win - dow.

Oh,   John - ny,   aren't   you   tired?

IX-8

Composing with F

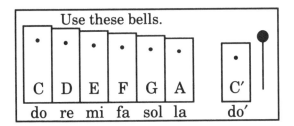

Use these bells.

C D E F G A C'

do re mi fa sol la do'

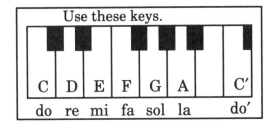

Use these keys.

C D E F G A C'

do re mi fa sol la do'

1. Learn to sing and play the first part of this song. Add notes above the words to finish the song. Sing and play the finished song.

Jack Be Nimble

Jack be nim- ble,   Jack be quick.   Jack can jump a   can - dle- stick.

If   the stick   is   up too high,   Jack can bake an   ap - ple   pie.

2. Compose your own song. Make your notes and rests on the staff below. Play and sing your song.

_____
Write your title here.

IX-9   **Congratulations!**

You have successfully completed Pack Nine. Write your name in the box. Bring this certificate to your teacher to have it signed.

GOOD   NEWS

We are learning to read music.

Write your name here.

has
successfully
completed
PACK NINE.

C O N G R A T U L A T I O N S !

_____   _____
Date   *Teacher's Signature*

Pack Nine Bonus Page

Make Up a Rhythm
A Card Game for You and a Partner

Directions: Find a partner who has also completed Pack Nine. Cut these cards apart. Decide who will be the pattern maker and who will be the player. The pattern maker arranges any four cards into a pattern. The player makes up and plays a rhythm for each note in the pattern. Exchange jobs. Play until each partner has had a chance to play five or more patterns.

Name _____   **Date** _____

X-1   **Learning About Dotted Half Notes**

1.   Chant this rhyme and keep the beat. Clap once for each square.

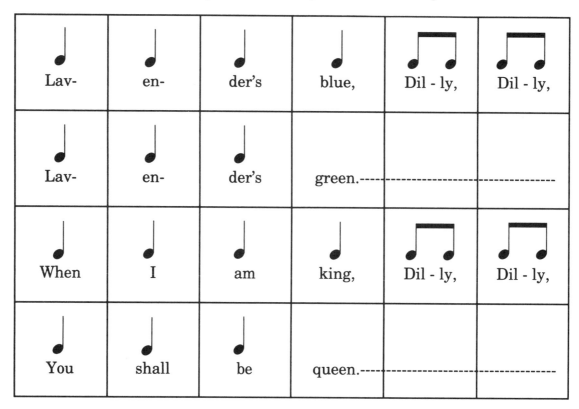

Every word square gets one beat. The word "green" gets three beats. The word "queen" gets three beats.

Some words last two beats. Some words last three beats. Musicians can write longer sounds with half notes and dotted half notes. A *dotted half note* gets three beats.

2.   Draw a dotted half note.

3.   Draw one *dotted half note* over the word "green" and one *dotted half note* over the word "queen" in the rhyme above. Clap and say the rhythm syllables.

X-2   # Reading Dotted Half Notes

Musicians can write longer sounds with dotted half notes. A *dotted half note* gets three beats.

1.   Chant this rhyme and keep the beat. Clap once for each square.

"Do,	re,	mi,	fa,"	is	the
Way	to	be-	gin.-------		
"do,	ti,	la,	sol,"	start	all
O-	ver	a-	gain.----------		

2.   Clap and chant the rhythm syllables.

♩ = ta   𝅗𝅥. = ta-a-a

Name _____   Date _____

X-3   **Writing Rhythm**

1. Chant the words to this rhyme and clap the beat. Clap once for every square.

♩	♫	♫	♩	♩	♩
Don't	throw your	dust in	my	dust	pan,
♩ My	♩ dust	♩ pan,	my	dust	pan,
Don't	throw your	dust in	my	dust	pan,
My	dust	pan's	full.------	------------------	--------

2. Finish writing the rhythm above the words.
    Add ____♩'s, ____♫'s, and one ____♩. .

3. Clap and chant the rhythm syllables.
    ____♩ = ta   ____♫ = ti-ti   ____♩. = ta-a-a

X-4   **Reading Rhythm Patterns**

1. Read and clap these rhythm patterns.

 = ta   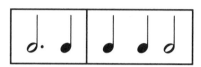 = ta-a    = sh

 = ti-ti    = ta-a-a

2. Write the correct rhythm syllables under these patterns. Clap and chant the rhythms.

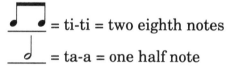

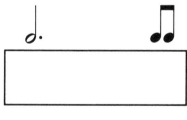

ta-a-a   sh

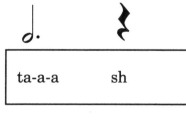

X-5

A Matching Game

Clap and chant these rhythm patterns. Match each pattern with the correct rhythm syllables.

1.

   ta-a-a   ta

2.

   ta   ta-a   ta

3.

   ta-a-a   sh

4.

   ti-ti   ta   ta-a

5.

   ta-a   ti-ti   ta

6.

   ti-ti   ta-a-a

X-6   **Playing Rhythm Patterns**

1. Read and clap these rhythm patterns.

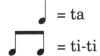 = ta   = ta-a   = sh

= ti-ti   = ta-a-a

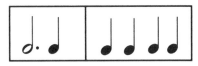

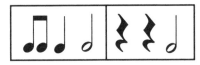

2.   Use a pair of rhythm sticks to play these rhythm patterns.

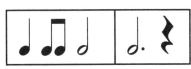

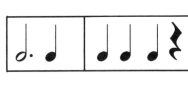

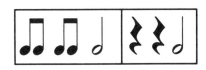

3.   Find a partner. You will each need a pair of rhythm sticks. Decide who will play one of the patterns above, and who will play the beat. Try to play both at the same time without getting mixed up. Exchange jobs and try again.

X-7   ## Compose Your Own Pattern

1. Compose your own rhythm pattern. Write your notes or rests in the squares below. Remember that a half note will take two squares, and a dotted half note will take three squares.

2. Practice clapping and chanting your pattern. Play your pattern on rhythm sticks.

3. Exchange patterns with a friend. Play your friend's pattern on rhythm sticks.

X-8   # A Song to Sing and Play

Play this song. Sing the words. Sing the syllables. Sing the rhythm syllables.

My Dustpan

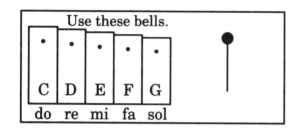

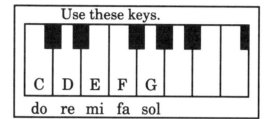

Don't   throw   your   dust   in   my   dust   pan,

My   dust   pan,   my   dust   pan,

Don't   throw   your   dust   in   my   dust   pan,

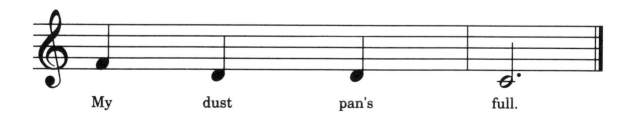

My   dust   pan's   full.

Name _____ **Date** _____

Congratulations!

You have successfully completed Pack Ten. Write your name in the box. Bring this certificate to your teacher to have it signed.

G O O D   N E W S

We are learning to read music.

Write your name here.

has

successfully

completed

PACK TEN.

C O N G R A T U L A T I O N S !

_____   _____
Date   *Teacher's Signature*

X-10   # Pack Ten Bonus Page

Create a Pattern - Game 4
A Card Game for You and a Partner

Directions: Find a partner who has also completed Pack Ten. Cut these cards apart. Decide who will be the pattern maker and who will be the player. The pattern maker arranges any two cards into a pattern. The player plays the pattern and sings the rhythm syllables aloud. Exchange jobs. Play until each partner has had a chance to play five or more patterns.

XI-1   **Singing Ti**

These notes can be named
do, re, mi, fa, sol, la, and
high do'.

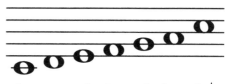

do re mi fa sol la do'

The line between *la* and
high do' is *ti*.

Your teacher will help you sing this song.

On St. Paul's Steeple

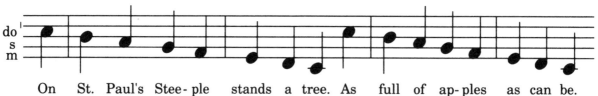

On St. Paul's Stee- ple   stands a tree. As   full of ap- ples   as can be.
do' ti la sol

The   girls and boys of   Lon- don town, they   run with hooks to   pull them down.

XI-2 # Finding Ti on Bells or Keyboard

The space between *la* and *high do'*
is *ti*.

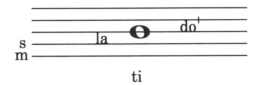

Play this song. Sing the syllables as you play.

On St. Paul's Steeple

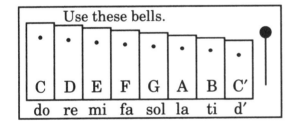

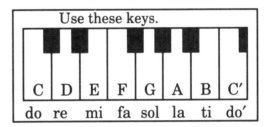

On St. Paul's Stee-ple stands a tree. As full of ap-ples as can be.

The girls and boys of Lon-don town, they run with hooks to pull them down.

Name _____   **Date** _____

XI-3   **Playing Ti**

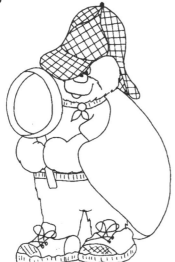

Study this song. Draw a square around every boxed[high do']. Draw a circle around every ⓣⓘ. Sing and play the song.

Miss Priscilla

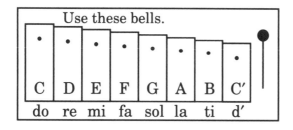

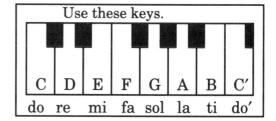

Miss Pris- cil- la,   she knew how to   milk the goat or   milk the cow.

Miss Pris- cil- la   had a dream to   chill the cow and   make ice cream.

Choc'- late,   van - il - la,   Miss   Pris - cil - la.

XI-4   **Learning the Treble Clef**

Music is often written on a five-line staff.

The lines and spaces can have

SYLLABLE NAMES   or   ALPHABET NAMES

do re mi fa sol la ti do'

C   D   E   F   G   A   B   C'

The treble clef sign
marks the *G* line.

The line between
A and *high C'* is *B*.

Write the alphabet name under each note.

B   A

XI-5   # Reading B

The line between
A and *high C′*
is *B*.

Play this song. Sing the alphabet names. Sing
the words.

On St. Paul's Steeple

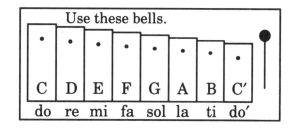

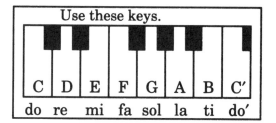

On St. Paul's Stee- ple stands a tree. As full of ap-ples as can be.

The girls and boys of Lon-don town, they run with hooks to pull them down.

XI-6   **Practicing B**

1. Make a pair of eighth notes above each letter.

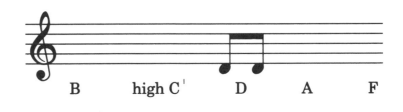

B   high C   D   A   F

2. Play this song. Sing the words. Sing the alphabet names.

Do Re Mi Fa

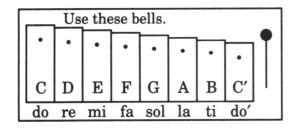   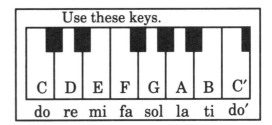

"Do, re, mi, fa," is the way to be - gin_____.

"Do, ti, la, sol," start all o - ver a - gain.----------

XI-7   # More Practice with B

Play this song. Sing the words. Sing the alphabet names.

Lavender's Blue

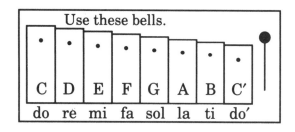
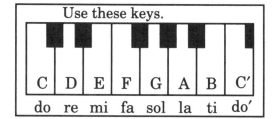

Lav - en - der's blue, Dil - ly, Dil - ly, Lav - en - der's green.

When I am king, Dil - ly, Dil - ly, You shall be queen.

Who told you so, Dil - ly, Dil - ly, Who told you so?

It was my heart, Dil - ly, Dil - ly, that told me so.

XI-8

Composing with B

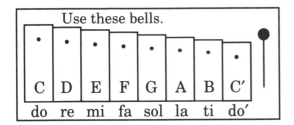

Use these bells.

C	D	E	F	G	A	B	C'
do	re	mi	fa	sol	la	ti	do'

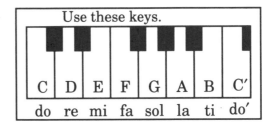

Use these keys.

C	D	E	F	G	A	B	C'
do	re	mi	fa	sol	la	ti	do'

1. Learn to sing and play the first part of this song. Add notes above the words to finish the song. Sing and play the finished song.

The Kite Song

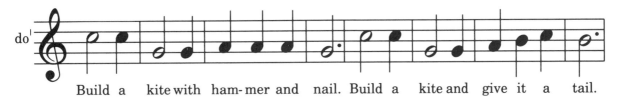

Build a kite with ham-mer and nail. Build a kite and give it a tail.

Build a kite and see how it flies, It'll take off in - to the skies.

2. Compose your own song. Make your notes and rests on the staff below. Play and sing your song.

_____
Write your title here.

Name _____ **Date** _____

Congratulations!

You have successfully completed Pack Eleven. Write your name in the box. Bring this certificate to your teacher to have it signed.

- -

G O O D   N E W S

We are learning to read music.

Write your name here.

has

successfully

completed

PACK ELEVEN.

C O N G R A T U L A T I O N S !

_____   _____
Date   Teacher's Signature

- -

XI-10 **Pack Eleven Bonus Page**

Name This Tune
A Game for You and a Partner

Directions: Find a partner who has also completed Pack Eleven. Cut these cards apart. Decide who will be the player and who will be the guesser. The player chooses one card, and plays it for the guesser. The guesser listens to the song and tries to name it. Exchange jobs. Play until each partner has had a chance to play five or more tunes.

XII-1   **Movable Do**

These lines can be named *do*, *mi*, and *sol*.

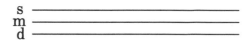

The do line can be marked with a key.

Do can move up or down. *Mi* and *sol* are above *do*.

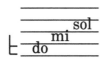   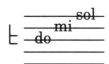

Do can be in a space. *Sol* and *mi* can be in spaces too.

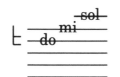   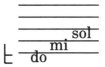

1. Circle the *do* key on each staff below. Mark the lines and spaces.

do = d   mi = m   sol = s

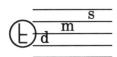      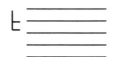

XII-2   # Reading Sol and Mi in Spaces

1. Circle the *do* key. Label *sol* and *mi*. Play and sing this song.

Cuckoo, Where Are You?

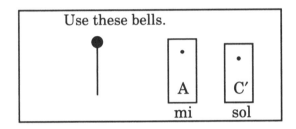

Use these bells.

A — mi   C' — sol

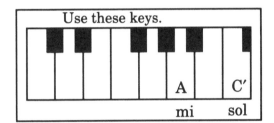

Use these keys.

A — mi   C' — sol

s   *m*

Cuck - oo,   where   are   you?   cuck - oo   where   are   you?

2. Read the treble clef and play "Cuckoo, Where Are You?"

Cuckoo, Where Are You?

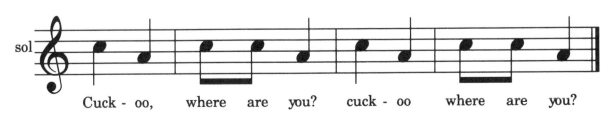

sol

Cuck - oo,   where   are   you?   cuck - oo   where   are   you?

Name _____   **Date** _____

XII-3      # Sol and Mi Songs

1. Circle the *do* key. Label *sol* and *mi*. Play and sing this song.

Seesaw

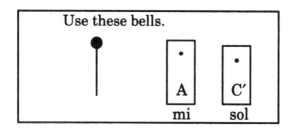   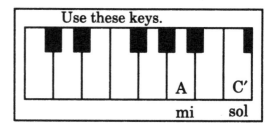

| See - saw, | smile | and | frown. | You | go | up. | I | go | down. |

2. Read the treble clef and play this song.

Chickadee

XII-4   # Reading the Treble Clef

Use the treble clef to help you play these songs.
Sing the words. Sing the alphabet names.

School Is Out

mi

School is out for to-day. Time to go out-doors and play.

One, Two, Tie Your Shoe

sol

One, two, tie your shoe. Three, four, shut the door.

Five, six, pick up sticks, Sev-en, eight lay them straight.

Nine, ten, a big, fat hen.

XII-5   **Composing with Movable Do**

1. Compose your own *sol-mi* song. Mark one space as *do*. Write your song on this staff. Play your song. Sing the syllables.

_____

Write your title here.

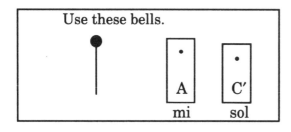

Use these bells.

| A | C' |
| mi | sol |

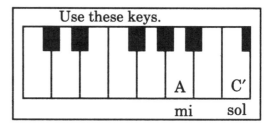

Use these keys.

A   C'
mi   sol

2. Rewrite your song on this staff. Play and sing your song.

_____

Write your title here.

sol = high C'   mi = A

XII-6

Where Is La?

The *do* line can be marked with a key.

Do can be in a space. *Mi* and *sol* can be in spaces, too.

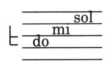 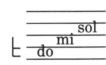

La is the line or space above *sol*.

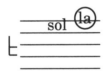 

Circle the *do* key on each staff below. Mark the lines and spaces.

do = d   *mi* = m   *sol* = s   *la* = l

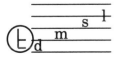 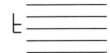  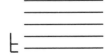

XII-7   # Sol, Mi, and La in New Homes

1. Circle the *do* key on the staff. Label *sol*, *mi*, and *la*.
    Play and sing this song.

Rain, Rain, Go Away

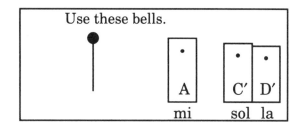

Use these bells.

A — mi   C' — sol   D' — la

Use these keys.

A — mi   C' — sol   D' — la

s   m

Rain,   rain,   go   a - way,   Come   a - gain   an - oth - er   day.

2. Circle the do key on the staff. Label *sol*, *mi* and *la*.
    Play and sing this song.

Bye, Baby Bunting

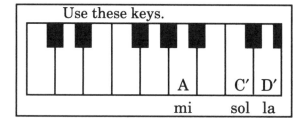

Use these bells.

A — mi   C' — sol   D' — la

Use these keys.

A — mi   C' — sol   D' — la

s   m   l

Bye,   ba - by   bunt - ing.   Dad - dy's   gone   a - hunt - ing.

XII-8 # Finding High D' on the Treble Clef

The lines and spaces can have
SYLLABLE NAMES.

These names *change* from
song to song.

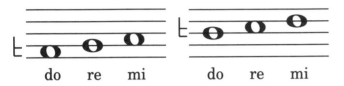

do re mi   do re mi

The lines and spaces can have
ALPHABET NAMES

These names *stay the same*
from song to song.

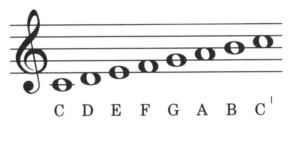

C D E F G A B C'

A New Alphabet Name

The line above *High C'* is *High D'* .

C D

D'

Write the alphabet name under each note.
Circle every (High D'). Draw a square around every [low D].

Sol Mi La Songs

1. Circle the *do* key in this song. Label
    sol, *mi* and *la*. Play and sing this song.

Rain, Rain, Go Away

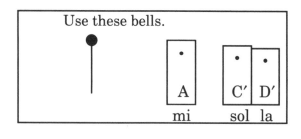

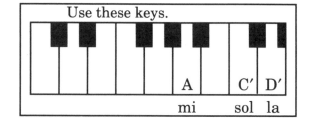

> *s* *m*
>
> Rain, rain, go a - way, Come a - gain an - oth - er day.

2. Read the treble clef and play "Golden Fish."

Golden Fish

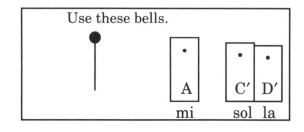

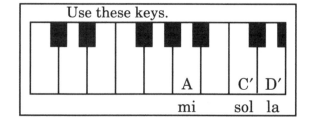

> sol
>
> Gold - en fish, gold - en fish, Can you grant one gol - den wish?

Name _____ **Date** _____

XII-10 # Reading the Treble Clef

1. Use the treble clef to help you play "Lucy Locket."

Lucy Locket

sol

Lu - cy Lock - et   lost her pock - et,   Kit - ty Fish - er   found it.

Not a pen - ny   was there in it.   On - ly rib - bon   round it.

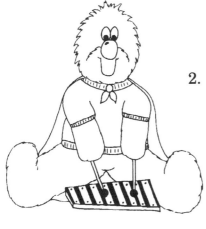

2. Use the treble clef to help you play this song. Sing the words. Sing the syllables.

Bye, Baby Bunting

sol

Bye, ba - by   bunt - ing.   Dad - dy's gone a - hunt - ing.

XII-11   # Composing with Movable Do

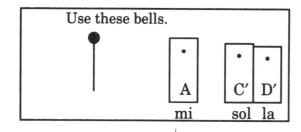

Use these bells.

A   C′ D′
mi   sol la

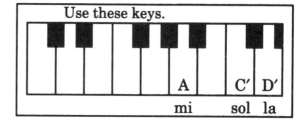

Use these keys.

A   C′ D′
mi   sol la

1. Compose your own *sol-mi-la* song. Mark one space as do. Write your song on this staff. Play your song. Sing the syllables.

    _____

    Write your title here.

2. Rewrite your song on this staff. Play and sing your song.

    _____

    Write your title here.

    mi = A   *sol* = high C′   *la* = high D′

Name _____ Date _____

Congratulations!

You have successfully completed Pack Twelve. Write your name in the box. Bring this certificate to your teacher to have it signed.

- -

GOOD   NEWS

We are learning to read music.

Write your name here.

has
successfully
completed
PACK TWELVE.

C O N G R A T U L A T I O N S !

_____   _____
Date   *Teacher's Signature*

- -

XII-13   **Pack Twelve Bonus Page**

Figure It Out!
A Game for You and a Partner

Directions: Find a partner who has also completed Pack Twelve. Cut these cards apart and place them face down between the two players. One player draws a card, looks at it, and shows it to the other player. Set a timer or check the second hand on the clock. Both players have one minute to figure out how to play the tune on the card. When time is up, the player who can play more of the song accurately scores one point. Play until one player has five points.

CUCKOO, WHERE ARE YOU?  Start on high C′.	RAIN, RAIN GO AWAY Start on high D′.
LUCY LOCKET  Start on G.	STAR LIGHT, STAR BRIGHT Start on F.
BYE, BABY BUNTING  Start on high C′.	ONE, TWO, TIE YOUR SHOE  Start on high D′.

XIII-1   # Using Black Bells or Keys

The lines and spaces can have

SYLLABLE NAMES   or   ALPHABET NAMES

do   re   mi   do   re   mi   C   D   E   F   G   A   B   C'

Each line or space can be played on one bell or key.

1.   Play this song.

Rain, Rain, Go Away

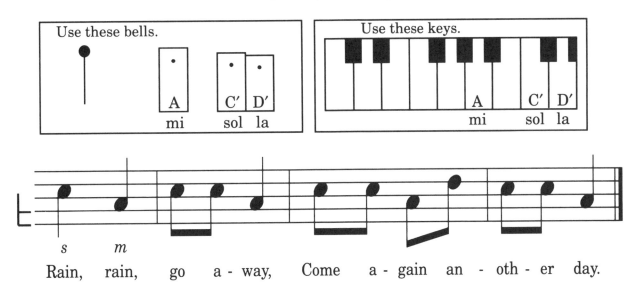

s   m

Rain,   rain,   go   a - way,   Come   a - gain   an - oth - er   day.

2.   Play this song again. *Sol*, *mi*, and *la* have moved!

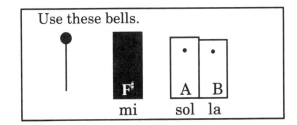
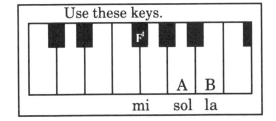

XIII-2   **Playing on the Black Keys**

1.   Play this song.

Golden Fish

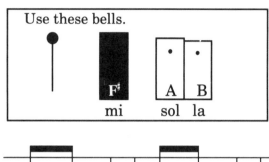

Use these bells.

F♯   A   B
mi   sol   la

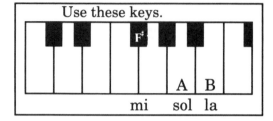

Use these keys.

F♯   A   B
mi   sol   la

Gold - en fish,   gold - en fish,   Can you grant one   gol - den wish?

The black bell or key in this song is called *F sharp*.

The symbol for *sharp* is

This note is *F sharp*.

2.   Circle every F♯ in this song. Play the song.

Bye, Baby Bunting

sol

Bye, ba - by bunt - ing, Dad - dy's gone   a - hunt - ing.

XIII-3 # Reading Songs with Sharps

1. Circle every sharp. Write the syllable names under the words. Sing and play this song.

Cuckoo, Where Are You?

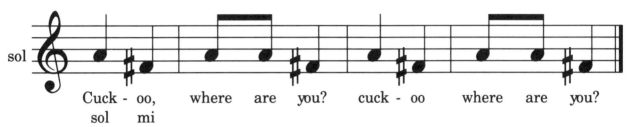

Cuck - oo,   where   are   you?   cuck - oo   where   are   you?
sol   mi

2. Circle every sharp. Write the syllable names under the words. Sing and play this song.

Peas Porridge Hot

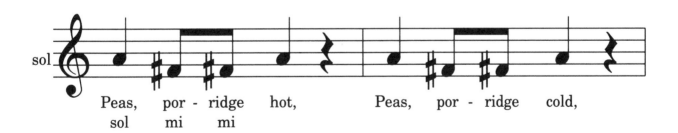

Peas,   por - ridge   hot,   Peas,   por - ridge   cold,
sol   mi   mi

Peas,   por - ridge   in   the   pot,   Nine   days   old.

XIII-4

You're Sounding Sharp!

Circle every sharp. Write the syllable names under the words. Sing and play this song.

Little Sally Walker

sol

Lit - tle Sal - ly Walk - er, Sit- ting in a sauc - er,
sol sol   la   la

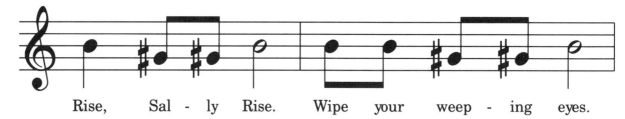

Rise,   Sal - ly Rise.   Wipe   your   weep - ing eyes.

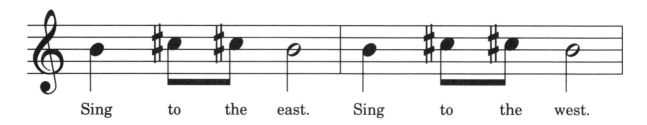

Sing   to   the   east.   Sing   to   the   west.

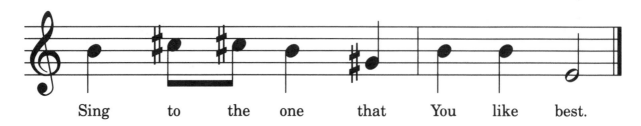

Sing   to   the   one   that   You   like   best.

XIII-5

Sharpen Your Detective Skills

1. This song is missing two sharps. Sing and play the song to discover where they belong. Add the missing sharps to the music. Sing and play the corrected song.

Ring Around the Rosy

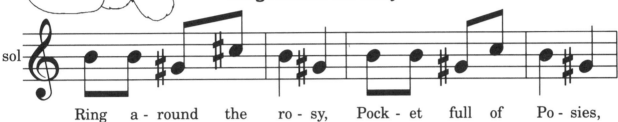

Ring   a - round   the   ro - sy,   Pock - et   full   of   Po - sies,

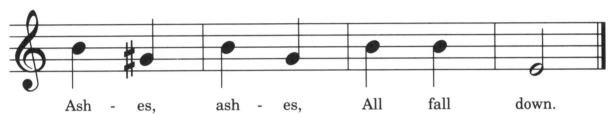

Ash - es,   ash - es,   All   fall   down.

2. This song has too many sharps! Sing and play the song to discover which sharps should be taken out. Cross out two incorrect sharps. Sing and play the corrected song.

Mary Had a Little Lamb

Mar - y had a   lit - tle lamb,   lit - tle lamb,   lit - tle lamb.

Mar - y had a   lit - tle lamb,   its   fleece was white as   snow.

XIII-6   **An Old Favorite — In Sharps!**

Circle every sharp. Write the syllable names
under the words. Sing and play this song.

Twinkle, Twinkle, Little Star

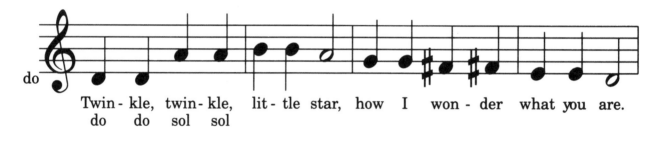

Twin - kle, twin - kle, lit - tle star, how I won - der what you are.
do   do   sol   sol

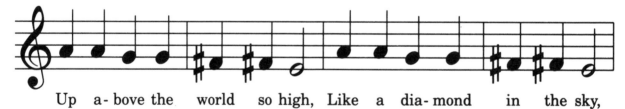

Up a- bove the world so high, Like a dia- mond in the sky,

Twin - kle, twin - kle lit - tle star, how I won - der what you are.

XIII-7   **Composing with Sharps**

1. Compose your own song. Mark one space as *do*. Write your song on this staff. Play your song. Sing the syllables.

_____
Write your title here.

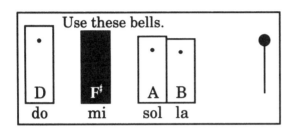

Use these bells.

D   F♯   A   B
do   mi   sol   la

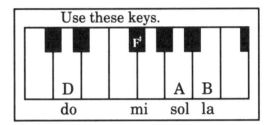

Use these keys.

F♯

D   A   B
do   mi   sol   la

(staff lines)

2. Rewrite your song on this staff. Play and sing your song.

_____
Write your title here.

do = low d   mi = F♯   sol = A   la = b

(treble clef staff)

Name _____   **Date** _____

XIII-8   **Congratulations!**

You have successfully completed Pack Thirteen. Write your name in the box. Bring this certificate to your teacher to have it signed.

G O O D   N E W S

We are learning to read music.

Write your name here.

has
successfully
completed
PACK THIRTEEN.

C O N G R A T U L A T I O N S !

_____   _____
Date   *Teacher's Signature*

Name _____   Date _____

XIII-9

Pack Thirteen Bonus Page

Name This Tune
A Puzzle for You and a Partner

Directions: Find a partner who has also completed Pack Thirteen. Work together to play each of the tunes on the page. Listen carefully as you play. Write the name of each tune in the blank.

Tune No. 1 _____

Tune No. 2 _____

Tune No. 3 _____

Tune No. 4 _____

XIV-1   # Using Black Bells or Keys

The lines and spaces can have

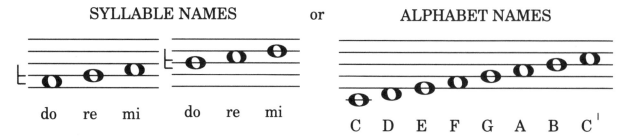

SYLLABLE NAMES   or   ALPHABET NAMES

do re mi   do re mi   C D E F G A B C'

Each line or space can be played on one bell or key.

1.   Play this song.

Rain, Rain, Go Away

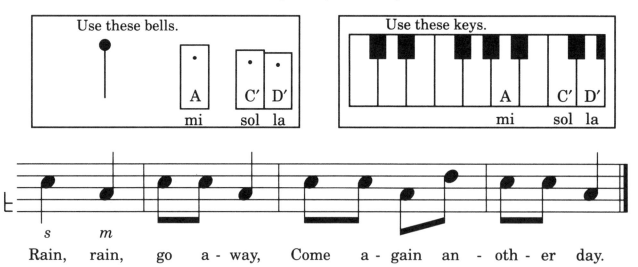

s   *m*

Rain,   rain,   go   a - way,   Come   a - gain   an - oth - er   day.

2.   Play this song again. *Sol*, *mi*, and *la* have moved!

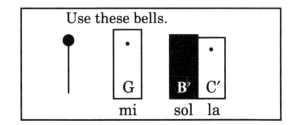

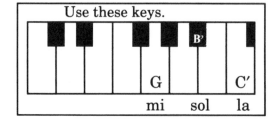

XIV-2   **Playing on the Black Keys**

1.   Play this song.

Golden Fish

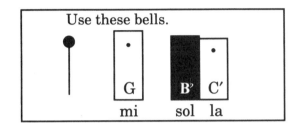

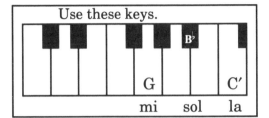

Gold - en   fish,   gold - en   fish,   Can   you   grant   one   gol - den   wish?

The black bell or key in this song is called *B flat*.

The symbol for *flat* is

This note is *B flat*.

2.   Circle every Ⓑ♭ in this song. Play the song.

Bye, Baby Bunting

sol   Bye,   ba - by   bunt- ing.   Dad - dy's gone a - hunt - ing.

XIV-3   # Reading Songs with Flats

1. Circle every flat. Write the syllable names under the words. Sing and play this song.

Cuckoo, Where Are You?

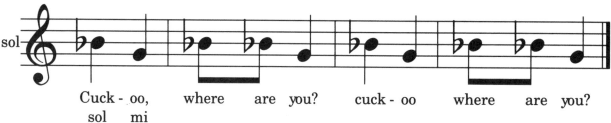

Cuck - oo,   where   are   you?   cuck - oo   where   are   you?
sol   mi

2. Circle every flat. Write the syllable names under the words. Sing and play this song.

Love Somebody

Love some- bod - y,   yes, I   do. Love some- bod- y,   yes, I   do.
do   mi   sol sol

Love some-bod- y,   yes, I   do. Love some-bod- y but I   won't tell who.

XIV-4

Flats Are Easy!

Circle every flat. Write the syllable names
under the words. Sing and play this song.

Rocky Mountain

Rock - y moun tain,   rock - y moun tain,   rock - y moun - tain,   high.
do   do   do   mi

When you're on   that rock - y moun - tain, hang your head and   cry.

Do,   do,   do,   do,   do   re - mem - ber   me?

Do,   do,   do,   do,   do   re - mem - ber   me?

XIV-5

Using Your Detective Skills

1. This song is missing two flats. Sing and play the song to discover where they belong. Add the missing flats to the music. Sing and play the corrected song.

Mary Had a Little Lamb

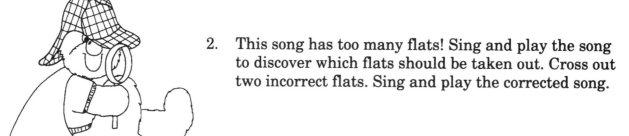

2. This song has too many flats! Sing and play the song to discover which flats should be taken out. Cross out two incorrect flats. Sing and play the corrected song.

Hot Cross Buns

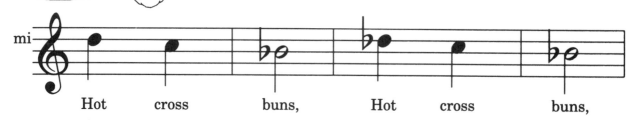

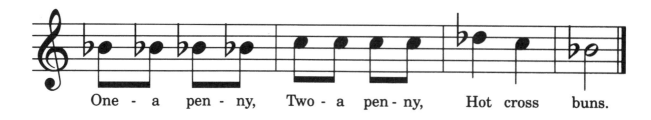

XIV-6   **An Old Favorite — in Flats!**

Circle every flat. Write the syllable names
under the words. Sing and play this song.

This Old Man

This old man,   He played one, He played nick-nack on my thumb,

Nick,   nack,   pad - dy   wack,   Give   a   dog   a   bone,

This   old   man   came   roll - ing   home.

XIV-7

Composing with Flats

1. Compose your own song. Mark one space as do. Write your song on this staff. Play your song. Sing the syllables.

_____
Write your title here.

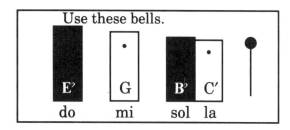

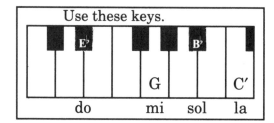

2. Rewrite your song on this staff. Play and sing your song.

_____
Write your title here.

do = E♭   mi = G   sol = B♭   la = high C

XIV-8   **Congratulations!**

You have successfully completed Pack Fourteen. Write your name in the box. Bring this certificate to your teacher to have it signed.

- -

G O O D   N E W S ♪

We are learning to read music.

Write your name here.

has
successfully
completed
PACK FOURTEEN.

C O N G R A T U L A T I O N S !

_____   _____
Date   *Teacher's Signature*

- -

Name _____   Date _____

  Pack Fourteen Bonus Page

Name This Tune
A Puzzle for You and a Partner

Directions: Find a partner who has also completed Pack Fourteen. Work together to play each of the tunes on the page. Listen carefully as you play. Write the name of each tune in the blank.

3

Teacher Resource Materials

- ANSWER KEYS
    - PACK ONE
    - PACK TWO
    - PACK THREE
    - PACK FOUR
    - PACK FIVE
    - PACK SIX
    - PACK SEVEN
    - PACK EIGHT
    - PACK NINE
    - PACK TEN
    - PACK ELEVEN
    - PACK TWELVE
    - PACK THIRTEEN
    - PACK FOURTEEN
- PACK TESTS
    - HOW TO USE THESE TESTS
    - HOW TO SCORE THE TESTS
    - REPRODUCIBLE TESTS, PACKS I–XIV
    - TEST ANSWER KEYS

- HOW TO EXTEND THE LEARNING EXPERIENCE
  - AESTHETIC EDUCATION THROUGH MUSIC READING
  - ACTIVITIES
  - ENRICHING THE LEARNING PROCESS
  - PERFORMANCES
- FOLLOW-UP ACTIVITIES
  - ADDITIONAL TEACHING AIDS
  - KEYBOARD GUIDES
  - HOLIDAY RONDO: A SAMPLE PERFORMANCE PLAN
  - BELL CHECKOUT CERTIFICATE
  - SUPPLEMENTARY SONG BOOK
- INDICES
  - ALPHABETICAL INDEX OF SONGS
  - TONAL INDEX OF SONGS

ANSWER KEYS

Pack One

I-6 Writing Rhythm

1.

Cuck -	oo,	Where are	you?
Cuck -	oo,	Where are	you?

2.

Star	Light,	Star	bright,
First	star I	see to-	night,
Wish I	may,	Wish I	might,
Have the	wish I	Wish to-	night.

I-7 Reading and Writing Rhythm

1.

One,	two,	tie your	shoe.
Three,	four,	shut the	door.
Five,	six,	pick up	sticks.
Sev - en	eight,	lay them	straight.
Nine,	ten, a	big, fat	hen

163

I-8 Names Have Rhythm

1.

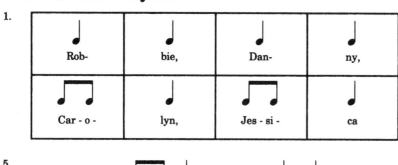

Rob-	bie,	Dan-	ny,
Car - o -	lyn,	Jes - si -	ca

5.

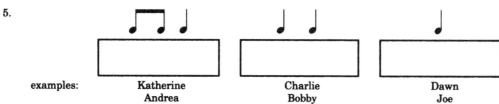

examples: Katherine   Charlie   Dawn
               Andrea   Bobby   Joe

I-9 Names of States Have Rhythm

1.

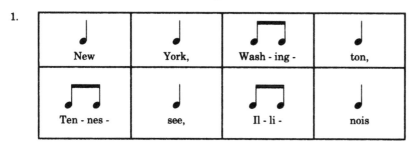

New	York,	Wash - ing -	ton,
Ten - nes -	see,	Il - li -	nois

5.

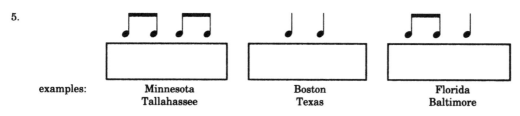

examples: Minnesota   Boston   Florida
             Tallahassee   Texas   Baltimore

I-10 Reading Rhythm Patterns

2.

ta	ta	ta	ta
ti-ti	ti-ti	ta	ta

ti-ti	ta	ti-ti	ta

ta	ti-ti	ta	ta

ta	ti-ti	ti-ti	ta

ta	ta	ti-ti	ta

ti-ti	ta	ta	ta

ti-ti	ti-ti	ti-ti	ti-ti

ti-ti	ti-ti	ti-ti	ta

164

I-11 A Matching Game

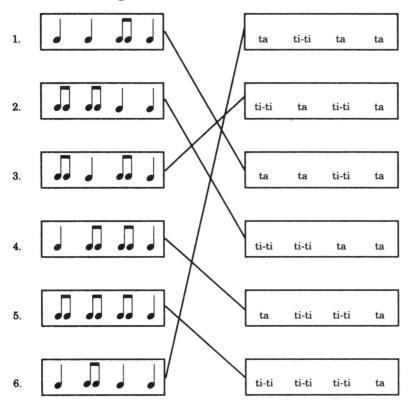

Pack Two

II-1 How Music Moves

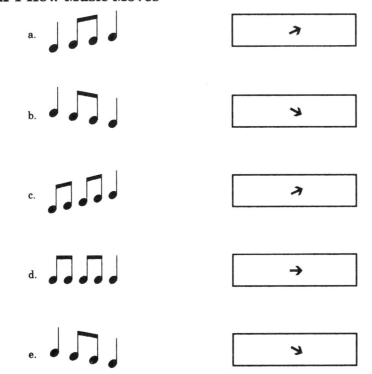

II-2 Up, Down, and the Same

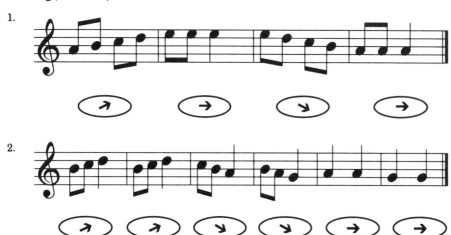

II-3 Line Notes and Space Notes

II-6 Playing Sol and Mi

II-7 The Five-Line Staff

II-8 The Treble Clef

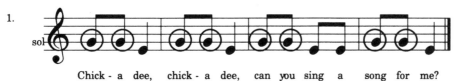

II-9 Reading G and E

 2.

Pack Three

III-1 Learning About Rests

1.

Peas	porridge	hot.	𝄽
Peas	porridge	cold.	𝄽
Peas	porridge	in the	pot
Nine	days	old.	𝄽

2.

𝄽

III-3 Writing Rhythm

1.

Ding	dong	dell	𝄽
Kit-ty's	in the	well	𝄽
Who	put her	in?	𝄽
Lit-tle	John-ny	Green.	𝄽
Who	pulled her	out?	𝄽
Lit-tle	Tom-my	Stout.	𝄽

III-4 Reading Rhythm Patterns

2.

| ta | ta | ti-ti | ta |

| ti-ti | ta | ti-ti | sh |

| ta | sh | ti-ti | ta |

| ta | ta | ti-ti | ta |

| ti-ti | ti-ti | ta | sh |

| ta | sh | sh | sh |

| ta | ti-ti | ta | sh |

| ti-ti | ti-ti | ta | ta |

III-5 A Matching Game

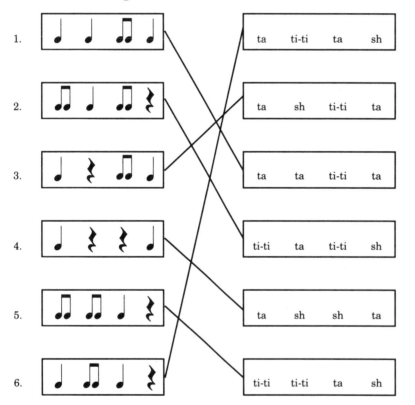

1.

| ta | ti-ti | ta | sh |

2.

| ta | sh | ti-ti | ta |

3.

| ta | ta | ti-ti | ta |

4.

| ti-ti | ta | ti-ti | sh |

5.

| ta | sh | sh | ta |

6.

| ti-ti | ti-ti | ta | sh |

Pack Four

IV-3 Playing Sol, Mi, and La

1.

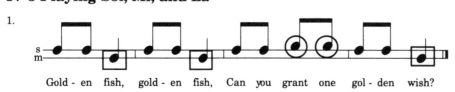

Gold - en fish, gold - en fish, Can you grant one gol - den wish?

IV-4 Learning the Treble Clef

G   A   E   A   G   E   G   A   A

IV-6 Practicing A

1.

A   G   E   G   A   E

Pack Five

V-1 Learning About Half Notes

1.

Mar - y	had a	lit - tle	lamb,
Lit - tle	lamb,	lit - tle	lamb.
Mar - y	had a	lit - tle	lamb, its
fleece was	white as	snow----------------------	

2.

V-3 Writing Rhythm

1.

Ring a -	round the	ro-	sy,
Pock - et	full of	po-	sies,
Ash-	es,	Ash-	es,
All	fall	down.----------------------	

V-4 Reading Rhythm Patterns

2.

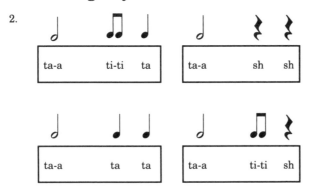

| ta-a | ti-ti | ta |

| ta-a | sh | sh |

| ta-a | ta | ta |

| ta-a | ti-ti | sh |

V-5 A Matching Game

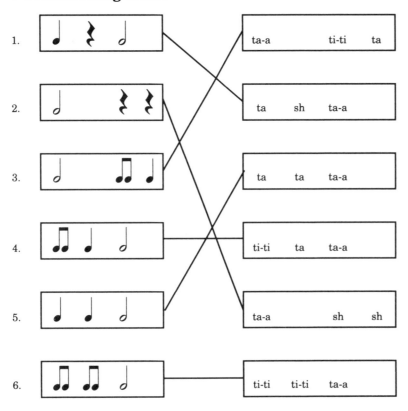

1.

2.

3.

4.

5.

6.

| ta-a | ti-ti | ta |

| ta | sh | ta-a |

| ta | ta | ta-a |

| ti-ti | ta | ta-a |

| ta-a | sh | sh |

| ti-ti | ti-ti | ta-a |

Pack Six

VI-3 Playing Do

1.

Moth - er's call - ing, Can't you hear her?

Moth - er's call - ing, Time to go.

170

VI-4 Learning the Treble Clef

G   A   E   C   G   E   C   A   A   C

VI-6 Practicing C

1.

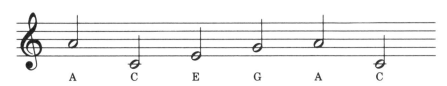

A   C   E   G   A   C

Pack Seven

VII-3 Playing Re

1.

Sing   a - round   the   camp - fire,   camp - fire,   camp - fire,

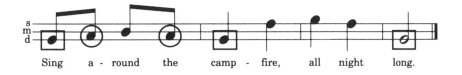

Sing   a - round   the   camp - fire,   all   night   long.

VII-4 Learning the Treble Clef

A   D   E   G   C   D   A   G   C   D

VII-6 Practicing D

1.

D   C   E   G   A   D

171

Pack Eight

VIII-3 Playing High Do'

1.

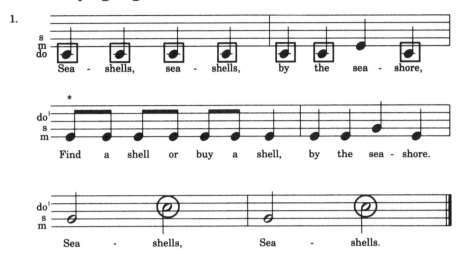

Sea - shells, sea - shells, by the sea - shore,

Find a shell or buy a shell, by the sea - shore.

Sea - shells, Sea - shells.

VIII-4 Learning the Treble Clef

C' A G E A D C C' C' A D

VIII-6 Practicing High C'

1.

G high C' E A high C' D

Pack Nine

IX-3 Playing Fa

1.

Love some - bod - y, yes, I do. Love some - bod - y, yes, I do.

Love some - bod - y, yes, I do. Love some - bod - y but I won't tell who.

172

IX-4 Learning the Treble Clef

F G C D E A C' A G E D C F C

IX-6 Practicing F

1.

D   high C'   F   A

Pack Ten

X-1 Learning About Dotted Half Notes

1.

Lav-	en-	der's	blue	Dil - ly,	Dil - ly,
Lav-	en-	der's	green.--------		
When	I	am	king,	Dil - ly,	Dil - ly,
You	shall	be	queen.--------		

2.

X-3 Writing Rhythm

1.

Don't	throw your	dust in	my	dust	pan,
My	dust	pan,	my	dust	pan,
Don't	throw your	dust in	my	dust	pan,
My	dust	pan's	full.--------		

173

X-4 Reading Rhythm Patterns

2.

X-5 A Matching Game

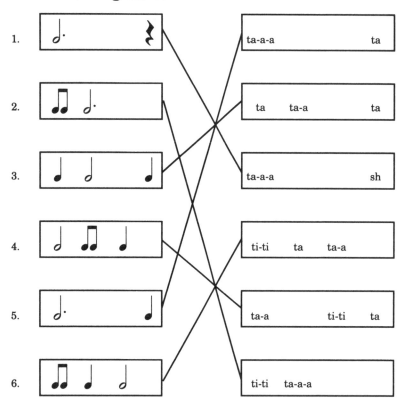

Pack Eleven
XI-3 Playing Ti

174

XI-4 Learning the Treble Clef

B A C C¹ E B D C G A B F C¹

XI-6 Practicing B

1.

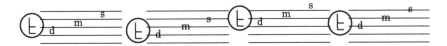

B high C¹ D A F

Pack Twelve

XII-1 Movable Do

XII-2 Reading Sol and Mi in Spaces

1.

s *m*

Cuck - oo, where are you? cuck - oo where are you?

XII-3 Sol and Mi Songs

1.

s *m*

See - saw, smile and frown. You go up. I go down.

XII-6 Where Is La?

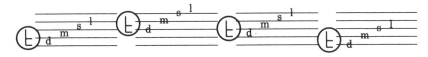

175

XII-7 Sol, Mi, and La in New Homes

1.

Rain, rain, go a - way, Come a - gain an - oth - er day.

2.

Bye, ba - by bunt - ing. Dad - dy's gone a - hunt - ing.

XII-8 Finding High D' on the Treble Clef

C' D' A D' D B G F E D C C' B D' D

Pack Thirteen

XIII-2 Playing on the Black Keys

2.

Bye, ba - by bunt - ing. Dad - dy's gone a - hunt - ing.

XIII-3 Reading Songs with Sharps

1.

Cuck - oo, where are you? cuck - oo where are you?
sol mi sol sol mi sol mi sol sol mi

2.

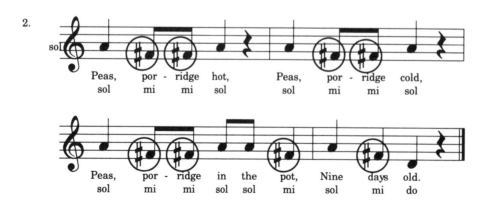

Peas, por - ridge hot, Peas, por - ridge cold,
sol mi mi sol sol mi mi sol

Peas, por - ridge in the pot, Nine days old.
sol mi mi sol sol mi sol mi do

XIII-4 You're Sounding Sharp!

Lit - tle   Sal - ly   Walk - er,   Sit - ting   in   a   sauc - er,
sol sol   la   la   sol   mi   sol sol   la   la   sol   mi

Rise,   Sal - ly   Rise.   Wipe   your   weep - ing   eyes.
sol   mi   mi   sol   sol   sol   mi   mi   sol

Sing   to   the   east.   Sing   to   the   west.
sol   la   la   sol   sol   la   la   sol

Sing   to   the   one   that   You   like   best.
sol   la   la   sol   mi   sol   sol   do

XIII-5 Sharpen Your Detective Skills

1.

Ring   a - round   the   ro - sy,   Pock - et   full   of   po - sies,

Ash - es,   ash - es,   All   fall   down.

2.

Mar - y   had   a   lit - tle   lamb,   lit - tle   lamb,   lit - tle   lamb.

Mar - y   had   a   lit - tle   lamb,   its   fleece   was   white   as   snow.

177

XIII-6 An Old Favorite—in Sharps!

Twin - kle, twin - kle, lit - tle star, how I won - der what you are.
do   do   sol   sol   la   la   sol   fa   fa   mi   mi   re   re   do

Up a - bove the world so high, Like a dia - mond in the sky,
sol sol fa fa mi mi re sol sol fa fa mi mi re

Twin - kle, twin - kle lit - tle star, how I won - der what you are.
do   do   sol   sol   la   la   sol   fa   fa   mi   mi   re   re   do

XIII-9 Pack Thirteen Bonus Page

Tune No. 1 "Mary Had a Little Lamb"
Tune No. 2 "Ring Around the Rosy"
Tune No. 3 "Twinkle, Twinkle, Little Star"
Tune No. 4 "Little Sally Walker"

Pack Fourteen

XIV-2 Playing on the Black Keys

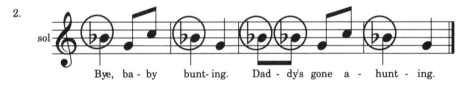

Bye, ba - by bunt- ing. Dad - dy's gone a - hunt - ing.

XIV-3 Reading Songs with Flats

1. Cuck - oo, where are you? cuck - oo where are you?
   sol   mi   sol   sol   mi   sol   mi   sol   sol   mi

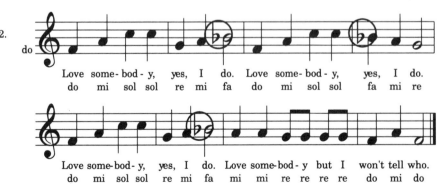

Love some- bod - y, yes, I do. Love some- bod - y, yes, I do.
do   mi   sol sol   re   mi   fa   do   mi   sol sol   fa   mi   re

Love some- bod - y, yes, I do. Love some- bod - y but I won't tell who.
do   mi   sol sol   re   mi   fa   mi   mi   re   re   re   re   do   mi   do

178

XIV-4 Flats Are Easy

Rock - y moun tain, rock - y moun tain, rock - y moun - tain, high.
do   do do   mi   do   do do   mi   do do mi   sol   sol

When you're on   that rock - y   moun - tain, hang your head and   cry.
la   sol mi   do   la   sol mi   do   mi mi re   re   do

Do,   do,   do,   do,   do re - mem - ber   me?
do   mi   sol   la   mi   mi   re   do   re

Do,   do,   do,   do,   do re - mem - ber   me?
do   mi   sol   la   mi   mi   re   do

XIV-5 Using Your Detective Skills

1.

Mar - y   had   a   lit - tle lamb,   lit - tle lamb,   lit - tle lamb.

Mar - y   had   a   lit - tle lamb,   its   fleece was white as   snow.

2.

Hot   cross   buns,   Hot   cross   buns,

One - a   pen - ny,   Two - a   pen - ny,   Hot cross   buns.

XIV-6 An Old Favorite—in Flats!

This old man, He played one, He played nick- nack on my thumb,
sol mi sol sol mi sol la sol fa mi re mi fa

Nick, nack, pad - dy wack, Give a dog a bone,
sol do do do do do re mi fa sol

This old man came roll - ing home.
sol re re fa mi re do

XIV-9 Pack Fourteen Bonus Page

Tune No. 1 "This Old Man"
Tune No. 2 "Hot Cross Buns"
Tune No. 3 "Rocky Mountain"
Tune No. 4 "Love Somebody"

PACK TESTS

Pack Tests are designed for periodic assessment of students' progress over and above day-to-day assessment. This section provides fourteen reproducible tests (one for each Pack of the series), teacher instructions, scoring suggestions, and answer keys.

How to Use These Tests

These tests give you the option of periodic informal assessment as students complete each Pack. Use them with individuals or groups. You may wish to follow this procedure:

1. Establish procedures and rules for testing.
2. Read through instructions for item #1. Allow time for students to complete item #1.
3. Read through instructions for item #2. Allow time for students to complete item #2.
4. Instruct students to practice items #3 and #4. Listen to and score individuals as they are ready to perform.

How to Score the Tests

Each test has a possible 10 points. Score as follows:

Item #1 (identification/recall)	=	0–2 points
Item #2 (comprehension/understanding) =		0–2 points
Item #3 (performance/application)	=	0–3 points*
Item #4 (performance/application)	=	0–3 points*
Total Score		0–10

*Prepare a scoring plan prior to testing. Decide what criteria will determine each score. For example:

Perfect performance	=	3 points
One pitch or rhythm error	=	2 points
Two or three pitch or rhythm errors	=	1 points
More than three errors	=	0 points (Student will repeat Pack or do remedial work)

Pack One Test

Name _____   **Date** _____   **Score** ____

☐   1.   Circle the pair of **eighth notes**. Draw a square around the **quarter note**.

♯   ♩   𝄽   𝄞   ♫   𝄪   ♩   ♭   ♩.

☐   2.   Finish writing the rhythm above these words. Write one **quarter note** or one pair of **eighth notes** in each square.

♩	♩	♩	♩
Star	light,	Star	bright,
First	star I	see to-	night,

☐   3.   Clap this rhythm pattern. Say the rhythm syllables aloud.

♩ ♩ ♩ ♩ | ♫ ♫ ♩ ♩

☐   4.   Play this pattern on rhythm sticks. Say the rhythm syllables aloud.

♩ ♩ ♫ ♩ | ♫ ♫ ♫ ♩

Pack Two Test

Name _____ Date _____ Score ____

1. Study this song. Draw a circle around every (sol). Draw a square around every [mi].

Chick - a dee,   chick - a dee,   can   you   sing   a   song   for   me?

2. Draw a quarter note around the *G* line. Draw a pair of eighth notes around the *E* line.

3. Play this song. Sing the syllables.

Use these bells.

E   G
mi   sol

Use these keys.

E   G
mi   sol

Cuck - oo,   where   are   you?   cuck - oo   where   are   you?

4. Play this line. Sing the alphabet names.

sol

Star   light,   star   bright,   First   star   I   see   to - night.

Pack Three Test

Name _____ **Date** _____ **Score** _____

☐ 1. Circle the **rest**. Draw a square around the **quarter note**.

♯ ♩(half) 𝄽 𝄞 ♫ 𝄼 ♪ ♭ ♩.

☐ 2. Finish writing the rhythm above these words. Write one **rest, quarter note,** or one pair of **eighth notes** in each square.

♩	♩	♩	
Ding	dong	dell	
Kit-ty's	in the	well.	

☐ 3. Clap this rhythm pattern. Say the rhythm syllables aloud.

♫ ♫ ♩ ♩ | ♫ ♫ ♩ 𝄽

☐ 4. Play this line. Sing the rhythm syllables.

sol

One o' - clock, two o' - clock, now it is three.

Pack Four Test

1. Study this song. Draw a circle around every (la). Draw a square around every [mi].

Gold - en fish, gold - en fish, Can you grant one gol - den wish?

2. Draw a quarter note around the *E* line. Draw a pair of eighth notes in the *A* space.

3. Play this song. Sing the syllables.

Use these bells.

E   G   A
mi   sol   la

Use these keys.

E   G   A
mi   sol   la

Rain, rain, go a - way. Come a - gain an - oth - er day.

4. Play this line. Sing the alphabet names.

Bye, ba - by bunt - ing, Dad - dy's gone a - hunt - ing.

Pack Five Test

Name _____ **Date** _____ **Score** ____

1. Circle the **half note**. Draw a square around the **rest**.

♯ ♩ 𝄽 𝄞 ♫ 𝄼 ♪ ♭ ♩.

2. Finish writing the rhythm above these words. Add **rests**, **quarter notes**, **eighth notes**, or **half notes**.

Bell	hor-ses,	bell	hor-ses,
Whats's the	time of	day? -------	-------------

3. Clap this rhythm pattern. Say the rhythm syllables aloud.

4. Play this line. Sing the rhythm syllables.

sol

Bell hors - es, bell hors - es, What's the time of day?

Pack Six Test

Name _____ **Date** _____ **Score** _____

1. Study this line. Draw a circle around every (do). Draw a square around every la.

Sing   to   the   one   that   you   like   best.

2. Draw a half note around the *C* line. Draw a quarter note in the *A* space.

3. Play this song. Sing the syllables.

Use these bells.

C   E   G
do   mi   sol

Use these keys.

C   E   G
do   mi   sol

Peas,   por - ridge   in   the   pot,   Nine   days   old.

4. Play this line. Sing the alphabet names.

sol

Sing   to   the   one   that   you   like   best.

Pack Seven Test

Name _____ **Date** _____ **Score** _____

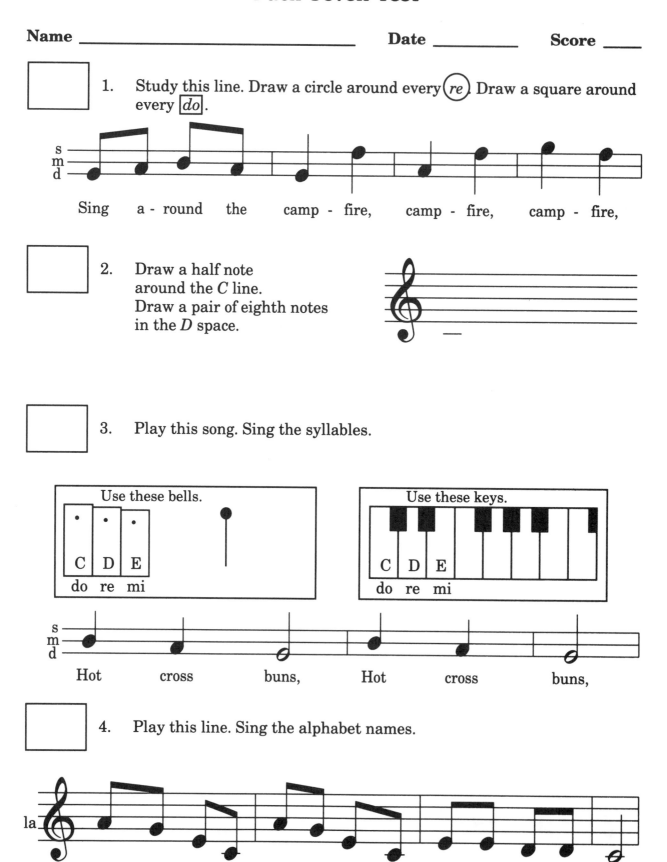

1. Study this line. Draw a circle around every (re) Draw a square around every do .

Sing a - round the camp - fire, camp - fire, camp - fire,

2. Draw a half note around the *C* line. Draw a pair of eighth notes in the *D* space.

3. Play this song. Sing the syllables.

Use these bells.

C D E
do re mi

Use these keys.

C D E
do re mi

Hot cross buns, Hot cross buns,

4. Play this line. Sing the alphabet names.

When you're on that rock - y moun - tain, hang your head and cry.

Pack Eight Test

Name _____ Date _____ Score _____

1. Study this line. Draw a circle around every (high do'). Draw a square around every [re].

Fed   my   cat   un - der   yon - der   tree.

2. Draw a quarter note in the *D* space.
Draw a half note in the *high C'* space.

3. Play this line. Sing the syllables.

Use these bells.

C	D	E	G	A	C'
do	re	mi	sol	la	do'

Use these keys.

C	D	E	G	A	C'
do	re	mi	sol	la	do'

Bought   me   a   cat   and   the   cat   pleased   me.

4. Play this line. Sing the alphabet names.

Ti - dee - o,   Ti - dee - o,   Close that win- dow,   Ti - dee - o.

Pack Nine Test

Name _____   **Date** _____   **Score** _____

1. Study this line. Draw a circle around every (fa). Draw a square around every [re].

This old man,   He played one,   He played nick - nack   on my thumb,

2. Draw a quarter note in the *high C'* space. Draw a half note in the *F* space.

3. Play this line. Sing the syllables.

Use these bells.

C D E F G
do re mi fa sol

Use these keys.

C D E F G
do re mi fa sol

Love some - bod - y,   yes, I do.   Love some - bod - y,   yes, I do.

4. Play this line. Sing the alphabet names.

Twin - kle, twin - kle,   lit - tle star, how I won - der   what you are.

Pack Ten Test

Name _____ Date _____ Score ____

☐ 1. Circle the **dotted half note**. Draw a square around the **half note**.

♯   𝅗𝅥   𝄽   𝄞   ♫   ⊧   ♩   ♭   𝅗𝅥.

☐ 2. Finish writing the rhythm above these words. Add **quarter notes**, **eighth notes**, or **dotted half notes**.

♩	♩	♩			
Lav -	en -	der's	blue,	Dil-ly,	Dil-ly,
Lav -	en -	der's	green. --------	------------	

☐ 3. Clap this rhythm pattern. Say the rhythm syllables aloud.

♩ ♩ ♩ | 𝅗𝅥. | ♫ ♩ ♩ | 𝅗𝅥.

☐ 4. Play this line. Sing the rhythm syllables.

Don't throw your dust in my dust pan, My dust pan's full.

Pack Eleven Test

Name _____   **Date** _____   **Score** _____

[ ] 1. Study this line. Draw a circle around every (*ti*). Draw a square around every [*fa*].

do¹
s
m

On   St.   Paul's   Stee-ple   stands   a   tree.   As   full   of   ap-ples   as   can   be.

[ ] 2. Draw a dotted half note around the *B* line.
Draw a quarter note in the *F* space.

[ ] 3. Play this line. Sing the syllables.

| Use these bells. |
| C | D | E | F | G | A | B | C' |
| do | re | mi | fa | sol | la | ti | do' |

| Use these keys. |
| C | D | E | F | G | A | B | C' |
| do | re | mi | fa | sol | la | ti | do' |

d¹
s
m

Choc'-late,   van-il-la,   Miss   Pris-cil-la.

[ ] 4. Play this line. Sing the alphabet names.

sol

Lav-en-der's   blue,   Dil-ly,   Dil-ly,   Lav-en-der's   green.

Pack Twelve Test

Name _____ **Date** _____ **Score** ____

1. Draw a circle around the **do key**. Draw a square around the **treble clef sign**.

2. Draw a quarter note around the *high D* line. Draw a dotted half note around the *B* line.

3. Play this line. Sing the syllables.

Use these bells.

A | C' D'
mi | sol la

Use these keys.

A | C' D'
mi | sol la

sol

Lu - cy Lock - et   lost her pock - et,   Kit - ty Fish - er   found it.

4. Play this line. Sing the alphabet names.

sol

Bye, ba - by bunt - ing. Dad - dy's gone a - hunt - ing.

Pack Thirteen Test

Name _____ **Date** _____ **Score** _____

1. Draw a circle around the **sharp**. Draw a square around the **do key**.

2. Draw a sharp and a quarter note in the *F* space.

3. Play this line. Sing the syllables.

Use these bells.

Use these keys.

mi   sol la

mi   sol la

sol

Bye, ba - by bunt - ing. Dad - dy's gone a - hunt - ing.

4. Play this line. Sing the alphabet names.

do

Twin - kle, twin - kle, lit - tle star, how I won - der what you are.

Pack Fourteen Test

Name _____ Date _____ Score _____

1. Draw a circle around the **flat**. Draw a square around the **sharp**.

2. Draw a flat and a quarter note around the *B* line.

3. Play this line. Sing the syllables.

Use these bells.

F G A B♭ C′
do re mi fa sol

Use these keys.

B♭

F G A C′
do re mi fa sol

do

Love some-bod-y, yes, I do. Love some-bod-y, yes, I do.

4. Play this line. Sing the alphabet names.

mi

Mar-y had a lit-tle lamb, lit-tle lamb, lit-tle lamb.

Test Answer Keys

Pack One Test

1.

2.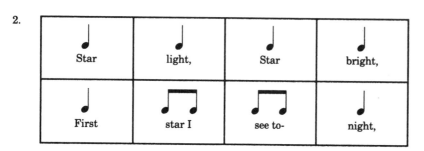

Pack Two Test

1.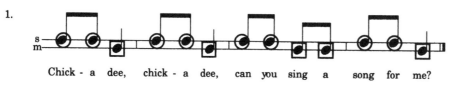

2.

Pack Three Test

1.

2.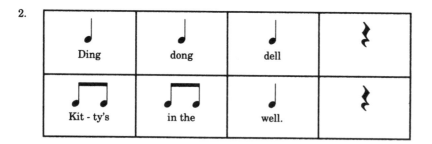

Pack Four Test

1.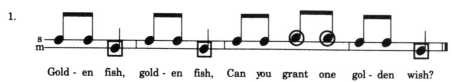

2.

196

Pack Five Test

1.

2.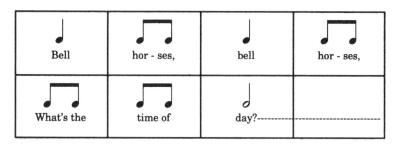

♩	♫	♩	♫
Bell	hor - ses,	bell	hor - ses,
♫	♫	♩	
What's the	time of	day?-----------	------------------------

Pack Six Test

1.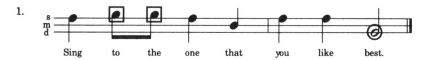

Sing to the one that you like best.

2.

Pack Seven Test

1.

Sing a - round the camp - fire, camp - fire, camp - fire,

2.

Pack Eight Test

1.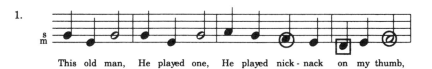

Fed my cat un - der yon - der tree.

2.

Pack Nine Test

1.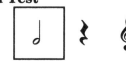

This old man, He played one, He played nick - nack on my thumb,

2.

Pack Ten Test

1.

197

2.

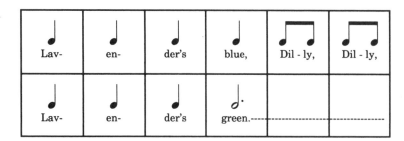

Pack Eleven Test

1.

2.

Pack Twelve Test

1.

2.

Pack Thirteen Test

1.

2.

Pack Fourteen Test

1.

2.

198

HOW TO EXTEND THE LEARNING EXPERIENCE

Reading music is an exciting process. The activities in this resource can be a catalyst for extending the learning experience. The following teaching suggestions include ideas for aesthetic education, ideas for performances, and ideas for using music reading skills beyond this series.

Aesthetic Education Through Music Reading Activities

The *Ready-to-Use Music Reading Activities Kit* can help develop musical and aesthetic awareness. Following are suggestions for aesthetic use of the activities. Stated in learner outcome form, these suggestions may stimulate your own ideas for creative use of the *Kit* for aesthetic education benefits.

The learner will . . .

1. Demonstrate F and P, crescendo and decrescendo.
2. Choose appropriate dynamic level(s) prior to performing.
3. Mark dynamic choices in printed musical scores.
4. Listen for dynamic levels while classmates are playing.
5. Experiment with variations in tempo.
6. Demonstrate FF, PP, and tempo variations.
7. Include tempo and dynamic indications in original compositions.
8. Experiment with differences in timbre between hard and soft mallets.
9. Experiment with timbre differences on a keyboard.
10. Experiment with various touches, attacks, releases, and the sounds which they produce.
11. Give examples of cadences that do and do not end on tonic.
12. Examine cadences of classmates' compositions and decide whether or not they end on the tonic.
13. Examine musical structure in a given folk song by:
    a. Finding two lines exactly alike.
    b. Finding two lines that are similar.
    c. Finding two measures alike.
    d. Finding two measures that are similar.
    e. Describing the form in letters.
    f. Labeling and performing phrases.
    g. Finding the musical cadence(s).
14. Create accompaniments on bells, keyboard, guitar, autoharp.
15. Create lyrics for a given melody.

16. Create an ostinato.
17. Add body percussion to a given song.
18. Create a percussion accompaniment to a given song.
19. Add an accompaniment to an original composition.
20. Combine two original compositions to create an ABA form.

Enriching the Learning Process

The supplementary songbook, pages 209–223, contains 14 reproducible songs, one for each Pack in this series. It can be used in several ways to extend music reading experiences.

1. Use the songs for extra practice or remedial help in the classroom.
2. Use the songs for enrichment in the classroom.
3. Make copies of the book available to students to check out and take home.
4. Reproduce enough copies of the book to allow each student to have his/her own copy.
5. Use the songs in performance.

Following are suggestions for extending and applying music reading skills beyond the scope of this series. These ideas may be used to challenge or extend the learning process for individuals or the entire class.

1. Use acquired music reading skills to sing and play songs from basal music texts.
2. Transfer music reading skills to another instrument, e.g., percussion instruments, recorder, flute, trumpet.
3. Extend composition skills on bells or keyboard.
4. Extend composition skills with a computer program.
5. Prepare a performance for a class of younger students.
6. Place keyboards and/or bellsets in the media resource center for students to check out. See page 208 for a sample bellset checkout form. Students can use the check-out instruments with the supplementary songbook.

Performances

The thrill of learning to read music is enriched when shared with others. Students will enjoy performing for each other in the classroom and performing more formally in public.

Solo *performances in the classroom* build self-confidence and peer group acceptance. Many teachers encourage solo performances during the class period. It is important to give students opportunities to be singled out as positive examples. Try an in-class performance day. Allow each child to choose a song and perform for the class as a solo or in a small group.

A demonstration of class progress in music reading can be an informative and impressive *performance for parents and the community*. Some options for program planning are:

a. An informal demonstration. Use a combination of large groups, small groups, and solos. You might include overhead transparencies created from the reproducibles, to allow the audience to read along and visually experience music reading with the children.

b. A more formal "concert" using exercises and songs from the series. Program a balance of large group, small group, and solo performances.

c. An open classroom visitation day. Parents, administrators, and the community are invited to observe and participate in a music reading day in the classroom.

d. See "Holiday Rondo," page 206, for a sample performance idea.

FOLLOW-UP ACTIVITIES

What a foundation you have built! Your students now have command of the basic elements of music reading. Where do they go from here?

The music reading skills developed to this point are a natural springboard to further music learning. Capitalize on your students' newly acquired skills and excitement for music learning. Initiate lessons on meter signatures, key signatures, other rhythm values, and other pitches. Follow the format of *the Ready-to-Use Music Reading Activities Kit*. Use musical examples to introduce and teach each new concept. Combine singing, playing, and other skills for hands-on application and reinforcement.

Suggested topics for follow-up lessons include:

1. Learning about the whole note
2. Music that moves in twos or threes
3. Identifying meter
4. Discovering meter signatures $\frac{2}{4}$, $\frac{3}{4}$, and $\frac{4}{4}$
5. Learning about other kinds of rests (half rest, whole rest)
6. What is an upbeat?
7. "1-2 and-3-4 ... ta ti-ti ta ta," which way is right?
8. Key signatures with sharps
9. Key signatures with flats
10. How to find *do*.
11. A new note: low *sol,*

ADDITIONAL TEACHING AIDS

Keyboard Guides

To the Teacher: Select a keyboard guide which matches the key size on your students' keyboard(s). Reproduce, cut out, mount on heavy paper, and laminate if desired.

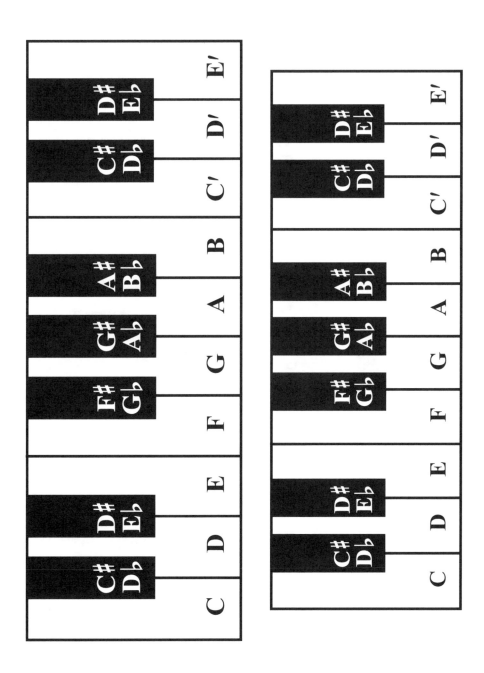

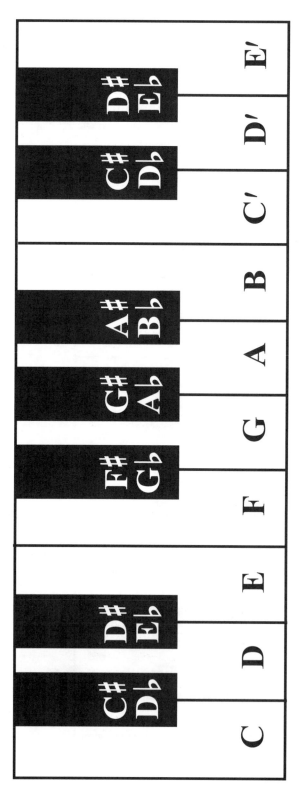

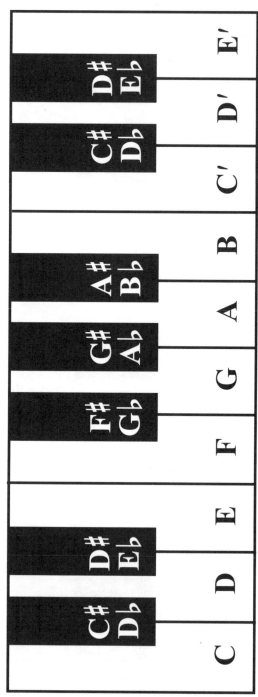

204

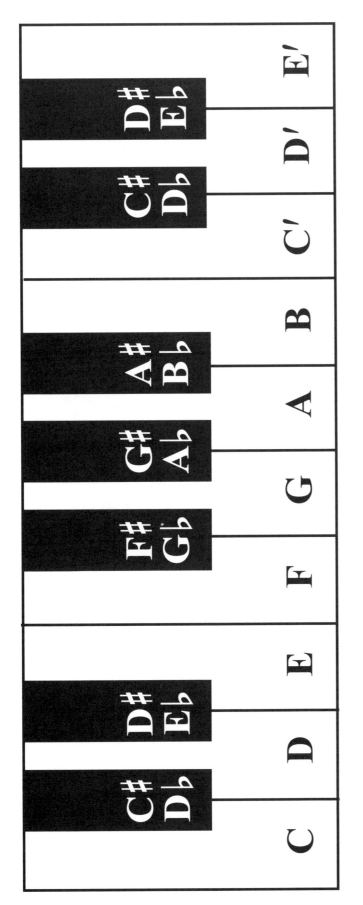

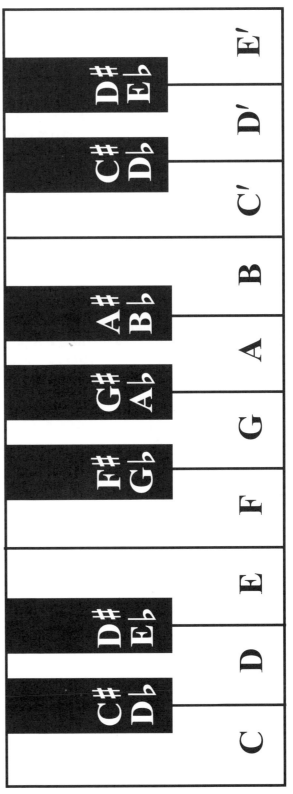

205

Holiday Rondo: A Sample Performance Plan

The following plan can be modified and used for seasons other than Christmas, e.g., "Halloween Rondo," or "Springtime Rondo."

Materials required: holiday songs
                                 instruments
                                 mural
                                 script for reader
Special assignments: reader
                                 soloist(s)
                                 small group(s)
                                 mural rollers

Reader: Our class has created a rondo combining several familiar holiday melodies. Before we perform it for you, we'd like to take a few mintues to demonstrate how a rondo works.

Let's compare a rondo to a series of store windows. First we have a window containing a lovely evergreen tree decorated with colored ornaments. We call this window the A part.

(Unroll mural to display Window A.)

Hol - i - day Ron- do,   la, sol, mi. Fol- low the hol - i - day rec - i - pe.

When our hol - i - day mu - sic's done, Come and join the hol - i - day fun.

Reader: We'll hear that tune many times during our rondo. Next, we will see a window decorated with candy canes. This is called the B part.
         (Unroll mural to display Window B.)
        *JINGLE BELLS

Reader: We will bring back the A part at this point. It's just like seeing the Christmas tree window again.
        * HOLIDAY RONDO

Reader: Now we need another new melody. We have chosen an original composition by _____. It is entitled _____.

(Unroll mural to display Window C.)
          *ORIGINAL COMPOSITION

Reader: Again the A part returns, followed by a new melody, the D part. The A part comes back after every new addition. We'll perform the entire HOLIDAY RONDO for you now without interruption. You might wish to follow our large musical map to keep track of the decorated store windows as you listen.

Here is a suggested sequence of melodies to include in a Holiday Rondo. This performance plan allows students of every ability level to perform successfully. The entire class might learn the A part, and small groups learn the other sections, according to their difficulty.

    A. *HOLIDAY RONDO*
    B. *JINGLE BELLS*
    A. *HOLIDAY RONDO*
    C. ORIGINAL COMPOSITION
    A. *HOLIDAY RONDO*
    D. *UP ON A HOUSETOP*
    A. *HOLIDAY RONDO*
    E. *JOLLY OLD ST. NICHOLAS*
    A. *HOLIDAY RONDO*
    F. *GOOD KING WENCESLAS*
    A. *HOLIDAY RONDO*
    G. *WE WISH YOU A MERRY CHRISTMAS*
    A. *HOLIDAY RONDO*

G O O D　　N E W S

Name

may check out a

☐ **BELLSET**

☐ **KEYBOARD**

_____
Date

_____
Teacher's Signature

G O O D　　N E W S

Name

may check out a

☐ **BELLSET**

☐ **KEYBOARD**

_____
Date

_____
Teacher's Signature

BRING A SONG ALONG

MORE SONGS TO SING AND PLAY

Pack One

Make instruments from things that you find at home.
Follow the key. Play each line on a different instrument.

Key:

two spoons	spoon and drinking glass	rice in a jar	hammer and wood

Good Night, Sleep Tight

	Good	night,	sleep	tight,
	Don't	let the	bed - bugs	bite.
	Good	night,	sleep	tight,
	Wake up	when the	sun shines	bright.

© 2003 Heritage Music Press, a division of The Lorenz Corporation

Pack Two

Good Night, Sleep Tight

sol

Good   night,   sleep   tight,

Don't   let   the   bed - bugs   bite.

Good   night,   sleep   tight,

Wake   up   when   the   sun   shines   bright.

Pack Three

Jack Sprat

sol Jack Sprat could eat no fat, his

Wife could eat no lean.

So be - tween them both, you see, they

Licked the plat - ter clean.

Pack Four

Snowsuits

sol

Mar - y, Al - ice, Char - lie, John,

Went to school with snow - suits on.

Teach - er said, "It's too soon.

This is just the month of June."

Pack Five

It's Raining

sol

It's   rain - ing,   it's   pour - ing,   the

Old   man   is   snor - ing.   He

Went   to   bed   and   he   bumped   his   head   and   he

Could - n't   get   up   in   the   morn - ing.

Pack Six

Eenie Meenie

sol

Ee - nie,   mee - nie,   mi - nie   moe,

Lost   my   step   and   broke   my   toe.

Doc - tor,   please,   will   I   sur - vive?

"Yes,   I   think   you'll   stay   a - live."

Pack Seven

Teddy Bear

Ted - dy bear,   Ted - dy bear,   Turn   a - round.

Ted - dy bear,   Ted - dy bear,   Touch   the   ground.

Ted - dy bear,   Ted - dy bear,   Show   your   shoes.

Ted - dy bear,   Ted - dy bear,   That   will   do.

Pack Eight

Fifty Nickels

Fif - ty nick - els, fif - ty dimes, and fif - ty cop - per pen - nies.

Fif - ty nick - els, fif - ty dimes, and fif - ty cop - per pen - nies.

Count and save, count and spend. Count some mon - ey for a friend.

Fif - ty nick - els, fif - ty dimes, and fif - ty cop - per pen - nies.

Pack Nine

Baa, Baa, Black Sheep

do Baa, baa, black sheep, have you an - y wool?

Yes, sir, yes, sir, three bags full.

One for my mas - ter and one for my dame,

One for the lit - tle boy who lives down the lane.

Baa, baa, black sheep, have you an - y wool?

Yes, sir, yes, sir, three bags full.

Pack Ten

London Bridge

Lon-don Bridge is fall-ing down, fall-ing down, fall-ing down.

Lon - don Bridge is fall - ing down, my fair la - dy.

2. Build it up with iron bars,
   Iron bars, iron bars.
   Build it up with iron bars,
   My fair lady.

3. Iron bars will bend and break,
   Bend and break, bend and break.
   Iron bars will bend and break,
   My fair lady.

Pack Eleven

Kookaburra

Kook - a - bur - ra sits in an old gum tree,

Mer - ry, mer - ry king of the bush is he.

Laugh, Kook - a - bur - ra, laugh, Kook - a - bur - ra,

Hap - py you must be.

Pack Twelve

Bobby Shaftoe

Bob - by   Shaf - toe's   gone   to   sea,

Sil - ver   buck - les   on   his   knee,

He'll   come   back   and   mar - ry   me.

Bon - ny   Bob - by   Shaf - toe.

Pack Thirteen

Taffy

Go, Tell Aunt Rhody

Go, tell Aunt Rho - dy. Go, tell Aunt Rho - dy.

Go, tell Aunt Rho - dy. The old grey goose is dead.

2. The one she's been saving,
The one she's been saving,
The one she's been saving,
To make a feather bed.

3. She died in the mill pond,
She died in the mill pond,
She died in the mill pond,
Standing on her head.

Alphabetical Index of Songs

225

Tonal Index of Songs

227

Ready-To-Use Music Reading Activities Kit
By Loretta Mitchell
Audio tracks created by Blair Bielawski

Using the CD

The accompaniments on this CD each have their own style and character, and we tried to give each track something special to tie it in with the lyrics. However, to make the CD easier for you to use, all of the CD tracks have several things in common. First, each track starts with a two-measure "lead-in" to establish the tempo and key. Second, most of the songs use the last four measures of the song as a tag to end. Third, most of the tracks from 9 – 21 include a short (two or four measure) interlude after the third chorus to give the students a chance to "re-group". We hope you and your students have a great time with the music!

Tracks 1 – 6 work with all the exercises in Pack #1:

1. Slow Rock (drums and percussion)
2. Medium Rock (drums and percussion)
3. Fast Rock (drums and percussion)
4. Slow Latin (drums and percussion)
5. Medium Latin (drums and percussion)
6. Fast Latin (drums and percussion)

Tracks 7 – 12 work with all the exercises in Packs #2 – 6 (using *mi, sol, la, do* and *re*):

7. Slow Latin (in "C")
8. Medium Latin (in "C")
9. Fast Latin (in "C")
10. Slow Rock (in "C")
11. Medium Rock (in "C")
12. Fast Rock (in "C")

The rest of the tracks are accompaniments to the *Bonus Songs* for each Pack that begin on page 210:

13.	Packs 1 & 2	Good Night, Sleep Tight
14.	Pack 3	Jack Sprat
15.	Pack 4	Snowsuits
16.	Pack 5	It's Raining
17.	Pack 6	Eenie Meenie
18	Pack 7	Teddy Bear
19.	Pack 8	Fifty Nickels
20.	Pack 9	Baa, Baa, Black Sheep
21.	Pack 10	London Bridge
22.	Pack 11	Kookaburra
23.	Pack 12	Bobby Shaftoe
24.	Pack 13	Taffy
25.	Pack 14	Go, Tell Aunt Rhody